Bengali Wins Freedom

Shahinul Khalisdar

Dedication

I dedicate this book to my beloved father and those who sacrificed their lives to protect Islamic culture after the 1793 Permanent Settlement Act and during the 1971 Indo-Pak war in East Bengal-East Pakistan (Bangladesh).

Acknowledgment

Writing a book from past memories is more complex than people thought and more rewarding than I could have ever believed. None of this would have been possible without the pandemic. Covid-19 was the first pandemic I have ever experienced. It helped me to be alone and remember the past.

I'm ceaselessly grateful to my project manager, Zara Morton, who took extraordinary care, allowed me to express my thoughts without boundaries and prejudices, and promptly responded to my emails.

The Second edition would not be possible without my account manager, Kevin. He advised me to redo "Reluctant Fathers" because his research showed some errors. Also, editor Michele, who handled the editing, saved my time and helped me deliver the best book.

I am deeply thankful to my father. He taught me discipline, tough love, manners, respect, reading, writing, maths, and more, which has helped me combat life. I genuinely have no idea where I'd be if he hadn't given me a roof over my head, as more than 2.7 billion people are homeless worldwide. I never regret being the son of an old man. I am always thankful to God that I had a great father.

I am also thankful to my maternal grandfather, Arshad Ali Choudhury, and Boro Ma. I used to call her "My" for their bedtime stories.

About the Book

Many people often asked me what motivated me to write the first edition of "Reluctant Fathers." To be honest with the readers, I need to admit that it was not my intention to write or publish the first book in the first place. In October 2006, I promised myself that I would never talk to Bengalis about Bangladeshi politics.

In 2018, I came to work in Alexandria, VA, for Block Advisor as a Tax Advisor. I was looking for a room to stay for the tax season next to a Masjid because, during the month of Ramadan, I frequently wanted to go to the Masjid, and for the last ten days, I was looking forward to staying in the Masjid.

In the Masjid, the hot topic was Bengali and **Bangabandhu**, and people were generally hateful toward Pakistanis rather than engaging in studying the Quran. In the month of Ramadan, they should have been talking more about the merits of Ramadan; instead, they were busy discussing the greatness of Bengalis. It felt pretty disturbing to me.

Secondly, I regularly went to a restaurant for lunch in Falls Church. In that restaurant again, Bengali and **Bangabandhu** were the highlights of all discussions, and the majority took part in hate speech against Pakistanis, which finally led me to make up my mind to write the book "Reluctant Fathers."

I would like to remind those who skeptically believe that Pakistan ISI or Indian RAW financed me to publish the books. No, absolutely not. No one paid me to publish the book. I paid from my pocket.

And those who skeptically believe that I am a Jaamati, for your information, I do not belong to any political parties or their political ideologies in Bangladesh or any part of the world. For that matter, I am an independent USA citizen and an ordinary Muslim born in a Muslim political family in Sylhet, Bangladesh.

However, I am the grandson of a Muslim League founding member and son of a late Muslim League leader, and that specific political background compels me to write this book. The "Bengali Wins Freedom" reflects on past political issues in the Indian subcontinent. I would like to mention that I do not intend to hurt anyone's personal feelings or emotions in writing about political, social, economic, and religious issues. I just want to make the history straight.

I intend to maintain an independent political perspective and neutrality free from political, religious, and cultural bias. That said, I am a born Muslim and have gained Islamic knowledge in the Aqeedah throughout my life, which might reflect, to some extent, in my writing.

I wrote this book from whatever I heard in my childhood. Then, I verified it by researching in public libraries to correlate to my existing knowledge of Indian subcontinental politics and found documentaries on YouTube and Google about Indian, Pakistani, and Bangladeshi political issues, actors, and events. I am confident this book is a practical and accurate historical political issue for both countries, Pakistan and Bangladesh.

Revised Edition

The first book "Reluctant Father" was based on my childhood memories from bedtime stories from my Boro Ma and my father's coffee table conversations with his friends, colleagues, and relatives, and my political discussions with some prominent political leaders and journalists from Bangladesh, India, and Pakistan during my Muslim student activism in the tri-state area. It is also important to mention that Dr. Shafiq, a former professor at Dhaka University from 1949 to 52 and a former scientist at New York-Presbyterian, retired in 2005. He advised me to write something on the Muslim League and Pakistan as I am a legend to people who may benefit from it. I responded that Bangladeshi Bengalis want to learn nothing except for the propaganda to hate Pakistani and be proud of being Bengali.

The book's "Revised Edition" is the same as the first and second editions, but I have added a few more events that I omitted from the first edition due to some advice from the editor and my well-wishers. And also removed Bengali words. The first editor did not fully understand my book's intended meaning because of our cultural barriers; that is why I redid the "book" with a new name, "Bengali Wins Freedom."

About the Author

Shahinul Islam Khalisdar, EA, MST, is the grandson of a Muslim League founding member and son of a late Muslim League leader by profession, a Tax Advisor. He was born in Sylhet, Bangladesh. He has been living in the USA for a very long time. And he has all his life witnessed political climate and media propaganda. Due to anti-Muslim sentiment skyrocketing globally, some people asked him to pen down as a grandson and son of a Muslim League leader.

Bengali Wins Freedom is Shahinul Islam Khalisdar's fourth book, renamed 2nd Book *Reluctant Fathers*, and the first book in Bangladeshi political science. He aims to bring the truth because Bangladeshi media systematically brainwashed Bangladeshi Bengali for the last 30 years. And portrayed Muslims as rapists, murderers, and foreign culture importers.

His main aim is to write a comprehensive book based on his personal experiences, which are straightforward and stick with the truth, facts, policy, and expert opinions. He has also written on LinkedIn, President Trump's Facebook page, Prime Minister Narendra Modi, Imran Khan, and Sheikh Hasina's son, Sajeeb Wazed. Behind the scenes, he advised dozens of high-profile Muslim country leaders from 1995 to 2006 in NYC on the critical political issues and foreign policy.

Contents

Page Blank Intentionally

Introduction

Since I was a toddler, I have heard about the 1971 War between Pakistan and India. That war is a source of pride for Bangladeshi Bengalis. It stands as one of the most significant achievements in the thousands of years of Bangladeshi Bengali history.

Bangladeshi Bengalis refer to it as "Hazar Bosorer Bengali." They passionately defend their Bengali identity and culture in restaurants, college cafeterias, and annual celebrations by publicly condemning Razakars, al-Badr, and al-Shams. This pride makes them feel more Bengali than Indian Bengalis as a whole.

On the other hand, the 1971 war was a significant setback for Muslim nationalists worldwide. In thousands of years of Islamic history, Muslims had never faced such humiliation. Nearly ninety thousand well-trained military personnel surrendered to the enemy and were taken as prisoners of war. I can sense this as the grandson of a Muslim League founding member and the son of a late Muslim League leader.

In reality, the '71 war was a victory for Indian military strategy, intelligence, politics, and foreign policy. India had invested millions in a smear campaign against Pakistan from 1948-1968 (the I.B. operation) and 1968-1971 (the RAW operation). They established a multibillion-dollar program for conventional and guerrilla warfare training for defected Pakistani military officers and soldiers, as well as recruited civilians for the 1971 war.

The foreign policy victory was evident when the USA refused to deliver military supplies to East Pakistan and an air-force fleet. The political triumph was realized in 1972 when Bangladesh crafted a constitution within the Indian doctrines.

I'm not entirely aligned with the founding ideology of Pakistan. While I respect Bangladeshi Bengalis' pride in being Bengali, I was also born in Bangladesh. With a thousand years of indigenous lineage in Sylhet, I feel compelled to share my analytical perspective in light of historical facts.

That's precisely why I've chosen to write "Bengali Wins Freedom." I'm fully aware that some Bangladeshi Bengalis may react negatively, but I believe that as the grandson of Muslim League founders, I can share their thoughts and historical accounts without fear of harsh criticism.

In 2006, I was in Iʿtikāf at the Jamaica Muslim Center, NYC. Upon my return, I discovered disturbing emails from former Muslim student activists. In Bangladesh, Bengali Nationalists had brutally beaten a Muslim activist to death while thousands watched. The mainstream international media remained silent, leading me to believe that the global media is biased against Muslims and has lost its moral consciousness.

I feel it's important to mention that I was writing a 32-page book on the hundred years of failure of Muslim League politics in the Indian subcontinent (Muslim League was founded on 12/30/1906, and 2006 marked a hundred years). On that day, I deleted the book and vowed never to engage in discussions about Bangladeshi politics with Bengalis.

I also have no intention of defending the Muslim League's politicization of Muslim nationalism in the subcontinent and the two-nations theory. The world has witnessed the pitfalls of politicizing Muslim nationalism.

I don't believe in coercion, as Allah (SWT) said: "There is no compulsion in religion; the right direction distinguishes from the wrong" (Al-Quran, 2:256). This book offers a comprehensive, direct, and straightforward perspective on political issues related to Bangladesh and its people. These opinions are personal, focusing on political actors and issue-based events. My aim is not to convince or convert anyone's beliefs about Bangladesh; everyone is free to believe what they wish.

On YouTube, bloggers express their viewpoints according to their own thinking. I will stick with bedtime stories, my dad's coffee-table conversations, YouTube documentary video clips, and the Quran and Sunnah. My intent is to remain free from biases and refrain from blindly defending anyone. The truth is one, and lies are ninety-nine.

Chapter One
The Bengal

I will briefly provide you with the history of Bengal, in line with the counts of Hindu historians. Hindu historians argue that Stone Age tools were found in the region, suggesting human habitation for over twenty thousand years. Remnants of Copper Age settlements, including pit dwellings, date back four thousand years.

In the following migration waves, people who settled in Bengal were identified as Austroasiatic, Tibeto-Burmans, Dravidians, and Indo-Aryans.

Hindu archaeologists claim, through evidence, that rice-farming communities inhabited the Bengal delta in the second millennium BCE. Rivers were used for transport, while maritime trade boomed in the Bay of Bengal. At that time, people were living in mud houses and producing pottery.

They also believed that "The Iron Age" saw the use of coinage, metallic weapons, agriculture, and irrigation. Large urban settlements were formed in the middle of the first millennium BCE when the Northern Black Polished Ware culture dominated the northern part of the Indian subcontinent. Alexander Cunningham, the founder of the Archaeological Survey of India, identified the archaeological site of Mahasthangarh as the capital of the Pundra

Kingdom, which was mentioned in the Rigveda.

The Rigveda is an ancient Hindu collection of Vedic Sanskrit hymns. It is commonly known as one of the Vedas, which are four sacred and recognized religious texts of Hinduism.

Hindu intellectuals have made the historical case that ancient Bengal is a part of India's history and also figures in the history of Sri Lanka, Siam, Indonesia, Cambodia, Burma, Nepal, Tibet, China, and Malaysia. According to the Hindu religious textbook, Mahabharata, the Vanga Kingdom, from which the name Bengal is derived, was located in Bengal. In Sri Lankan history, the first king of Sri Lanka was Prince Vijaya, whose ancestral home was in Bengal.

In the Greek-Roman Era, historians believed that the Gangaridai Kingdom represented Bengal. At the time of Alexander the Great's invasion of India, the collective might of the Gangaridai and the Nanda Empire (Bihar) prevented the Greek army's advances in India.

Archaeological sites like Wari Bateshwar and Chandraketugarh are linked to the Gangaridai kingdom. Ptolemy's world map places the emporium of Sounagoura (Sonargaon) in Bengal. Roman geographers also noted a large natural harbor in southeastern Bengal, believed to be the present-day Chittagong region.

In short, I have endeavored to shed light on the historical accounts of ancient Bengal to avoid any assumptions of bias, considering my Muslim background. There is no reason to undermine the thousands of years of Hindu history. The history books are readily available in libraries and online today.

Hinduism

Hinduism is an ancient Indian religion. According to Islamic belief, it is a polytheistic religion, which is contrary to Islamic monotheism. In the view of world religious historians, it is one of the oldest religions in the world. It is also the world's third-largest religion. Hindu intellectuals refer to Hinduism as Sanātana Dharma, which implies that its origins lie beyond human history. Hindu scholars view Hinduism as a self-designation of Vaidika Dharma, which is related to the Vedas.

According to my study, it is shown that Hinduism encompasses a range of philosophies related to shared polytheistic religious concepts from ancient to the present day. Recognizable rituals are shared between religions, as well as pilgrimages made to sacred sites and shared textual resources such as the Vedas. Many theologians, philosophers, and mythologists have discussed Vedic Yagya, yoga, agamic practices, and temple building as prescribed eternal duties. These include honesty, refraining from injuring living beings, patience, forbearance, self-restraint, virtue, and compassion, among others.

Hinduism has leading themes, which include the four Puruṣārthas, human life's reasonable goals or aims: Dharma (religion), Artha (prosperity/work), Kama (desires/passions), and Moksha (liberation/freedom from the cycle of death and rebirth/salvation). It also encompasses Karma (action, intent, and consequences) and Saṃsāra (cycle of death and rebirth).

Hindu practices include puja (worship) of nearly everything as a form of God, recitations of Shruti and Smriti, Japa and Dhyāna (meditation), family-oriented rites of passage, annual festivals, and occasional pilgrimages. Some Hindus, in pursuit of Moksha, practice various forms of yoga and renounce their social world and material possessions to engage in lifelong Sannyasa (monasticism).

The Hindu caste system is divided into four main classes: Brahmins, Kshatriyas, Vaishyas, and Shudras. Many believe these castes originated from Brahma, the Hindu God of creation. The Brahmin class is considered the top class, with "Brahmin" meaning "Supreme Self." It is the highest Varna in Vedic Hinduism.

Kshatriya is the second Varna within the social hierarchy and is understood to represent authority and power. This authority and power are not based on successful leadership but are inherited.

The Vaishyas are the third caste in the Hindu Caste System,

often referred to as the commoners. Hindu scholars defined Vaishyas as created from the storehouse of food (stomach) intended to be enjoyed by others.

Sudras make up the fourth or lowest class of the Hindu Caste System and are typically artisans and laborers. A significant portion of this caste results from the mating of an upper caste with an "Untouchable" or a "Sudra."

In cafeteria discussions, some Bangladeshi Bengalis strongly argue that they were forcefully converted to Islam from Hinduism by the sword. Conversely, some Hindus claim that the Sudras were converted to Islam through monetary incentives and marriage. I cannot entirely agree with Bangladeshi Bengalis because I am an indigenous Sylheti. I know that Muslim Mujahideen did fight against Hindu kings for various political reasons, but not with the intention of forcefully converting anyone to Islam.

There is no historical evidence to support the claim that Muslims forced individuals to convert to Islam in Sylhet. For instance, in Sylhet, Ghazi Burhanuddin was the first and only Muslim living there. When the Sultan of Lakhnauti, Shamsuddin Firoz Shah's army, defeated the Hindu King named Gour Govinda, Muslims migrated to Sylhet, and people reverted to Islam.

This war began when Ghazi Burhanuddin, the first Muslim living in Tultikar, sacrificed a cow for his newborn son's aqiqah (celebration of birth). In response, King Govinda had the newborn beheaded for what he perceived as blasphemy and had Burhanuddin's right hand chopped off. The general's army was aided by an Islamic scholar named Shah Jalal and his disciples and nephews. Chief Minister Mona Rai was killed in the battle, and King Govinda fled with his family.

The Kingdom of Srihatta was then renamed Jalalabad under the Muslim Sultanate. Sikandar Khan Ghazi, one of the commanders in the battle and Firoz's nephew, served as the first Muslim Amir (ruler) over Sylhet. Sikander ruled under Shamsuddin Firoz Shah for many years until his death, when a Hindu traitor sabotaged his boat, causing it to capsize and drown him. The Sylheti war is a true story that clarifies that Muslims did not initiate wars or forcefully convert the Hindus.

However, charity work in poor communities may inspire some impoverished individuals to revert to Islam. Nonetheless, this does not necessarily mean that all poor people in Bengal converted to Islam due to Muslim hospitality.

In conclusion, my aim is to present an objective perspective on the historical accounts of ancient Bengal without any bias as a Muslim. There is no reason to undermine the thousands of years of Hindu History. Historical records are available on library shelves and online resources for present-day access and examination.

Buddhism

Bangladeshi Buddhists hold various ideologies within Buddhism that may differ from the actual teachings of Buddha in modern-day Bangladesh. There is a folktale that suggests Gautama Buddha came to Bengal to spread Buddhism, while some Bengali intellectuals believe that one or two disciples came to propagate Buddhism in the region. However, Buddhism gained significant traction in the reign of Emperor Asoka, when it received political support. According to historians, the Pala Empire, which ruled the Indian subcontinent, played a pivotal role in spreading Buddhism in Bengal. Bangladeshi historians also mention a famous preacher named Atisha, who was born in Bikrampur during the Pala Dynasty and helped spread Mahayana Buddhism.

The 1202 War marked a significant historical event in the region. Historically, Muslim traders and preachers gradually migrated to India following the passing of Prophet Muhammad (PBUH). As Islam gained prominence in Bengal and Bihar, there were frequent tensions between Muslims and Hindus or Buddhists due to jealousy and envy. Muslims often sought justice from the Muslim rulers of Western India in response to these conflicts. As an example, the Sylhet War revolved around the significant issue of cows, which were revered by Hindus but considered a source of food by Muslims.

Ikhtiyār al-Dīn Muḥammad Bakhtiyār Khaljī eventually decided to take action against the local rulers in Bihar and Bengal. He made a sincere attempt to conquer Bihar in 1200, which led to a successful campaign and earned him recognition in the court of Delhi. In the same year, he turned his attention to Bengal. When he reached the city of Nabadwip, his rapid advance was so swift that only 18 horsemen from his army could keep up with the battles. In 1203, he conquered Nabadwip, wresting control from the old Emperor Lakshmana Sena.

Subsequently, Khalji captured the capital and principal city, Gaur, further advancing into Bengal. His successive victories against local kings facilitated the rapid spread of Islam in the region. Muslims in Bengal began to believe that Allah was sending angels to assist Ikhtiyār al-Dīn Muḥammad Bakhtiyār Khaljī in defeating the polytheistic rulers.

It is worth noting that Bakhtiyar Khalji's victories have been accused of causing significant damage to Buddhist establishments at Odantapuri and Vikramashila, which his army mistakenly believed to be fortified.

Historically, wars have always resulted in some level of destruction and damage worldwide, and this was no exception. There are credible historical accounts of war-related injuries and damage to buildings across the globe.

In the Chittagong Hills, Buddhist tribes constituted a significant portion of the population, practicing a blend of tribal beliefs and Buddhist doctrines. According to the 1981 census, there were approximately 538,000 Buddhists in Bangladesh, representing less than 1 percent of the population.

Muslim

Muslims are recognized as monotheistic individuals, belonging to one of the Abrahamic religions and practitioners of Islam. The Messenger of Allah has stated that "Islam is built on five pillars: testifying that there is nothing worthy of worship except Only One God and that Prophet Muhammad is the Messenger of Allah, establishing (five times) the salah (prayer), paying the zakat (obligatory charity), making the hajj (pilgrimage) to Makkah, and fasting in the month of Ramadhan." [Bukhari & Muslim]

Islamic history is distinct from that of other religions, as it does not involve debates among scholars or archaeological evidence to establish its authenticity. Islamic knowledge is derived from two authentic sources: the Quran and authentic hadiths.

For instance, Muslims do not accept the theory of random human evolution from apes. In Islam, human life began with the creation of two individuals, Adam and Hawwa (Eve). Allah created Adam from dust and breathed life into him. The angels were commanded to prostrate to Adam, with the exception of Iblees

(Satan), who refused out of arrogance. This event marked the beginning of human history. Allah created Adam's descendants and informed the angels that generations would follow on Earth [2:30]. Adam was also taught all the names [2:31].

When Iblees refused to prostrate, he was expelled and cursed by Allah. Iblees requested respite until the Day of Resurrection and declared his intention to mislead humanity[38:71-74]. Allah granted his request, and Iblees began his mission to lead Adam and his descendants astray.

The sin of Adam and Hawwa in eating from the forbidden tree was due to desire rather than arrogance. They repented, and Allah accepted their repentance [2:37]. Repentance is a fundamental concept in Islam, and sincere repentance is always accepted by Allah [42:25].

Allah sent Adam, Hawwa, and Iblees to Earth and continued to send revelations and messengers to guide humanity. The conflict between faith and disbelief, truth and falsehood, and good and evil began at this point [7:24].

In Islamic belief, Allah is the Creator and Designer of all, and He has created various creatures in unique ways. He created Adam without a father or mother, Hawwa from a father without a mother, and Eesa (Jesus) from a mother without a father. Allah created humans from a father and a mother, and their creation and development in the womb are described as wondrous in the Quran.

[32:7-9] [23:12-14].

Allah alone creates whatever He wills, knows what is in the wombs, and determines provision and lifespans [42:49-50]. Angels are appointed over the womb and record various aspects of an individual's life while still in the mother's womb [318].

The religion brought by Muhammad (peace and blessings of Allah be upon him) confirms the message of previous prophets and serves as a guide for all of humanity [2:213]. Islam calls for the worship of Allah alone and the rejection of all false gods. It emphasizes the oneness of Allah and the acceptance of His guidance.

The Quran and the authentic hadiths are the primary sources of Islamic knowledge. Muslims believe in the oneness of Allah, the prophethood of Muhammad, and the finality of the message. While Muslims may have different interpretations on certain matters, it is essential to adhere to the Quran and authentic hadiths to maintain unity and avoid religious tensions among Muslims and non-Muslims alike.

Prophet Muhammad predicted that Muslims would be divided into various sects, but he emphasized the importance of adhering to the main body of Muslims (jama'ah) [Hadith]. Therefore, Muslims must prioritize the Quran and authentic Hadith in their beliefs and practices. (Please note: above mentioned Quranic verses and hadiths are estimated translated intended meaning within American English Grammar. The original Quranic verses are **Mushaf Usmani).**

Chapter Two
Muslim Sultanate

The Muslim Sultanate began in Bengal with Bakhtiar Khilji's victory in Gauda between 1202 and 1204 during the reign of Muhammad of Ghor. After the Muslim victory, Sunni Muslims became the dominant power in Bengal. Following the assassination of Bakhtiar Khalji by the traitor Ali Mardan in 1206, Bengal fell under various Maliks (landowners), except for a brief interruption by Ali Mardan himself.

Until Delhi Sultan Iltutmish sent forces under his son's leadership to restore central governmental authority over Bengal, General Nasir-ud-din Mahmud successfully brought Bengal under Delhi's governmental control. Iltutmish declared Bengal as a province of Delhi in 1225. The Delhi government established a systematic governing capacity in Bengal by appointing Nawabs (governors).

However, Delhi couldn't successfully administer Bengal due to the distance and challenging communication between Bengal and Delhi. Disloyal governors rebelled against the Delhi government and declared independence, including my great-great-grandfather, who was recognized as a Mirasdar (Lord). Delhi's government militarily quelled the rebellious governors but recognized local Mirasdari.

Nonetheless, there were various self-declared rulers among the rebels, including Yuzbak Shah (1257), Tughral Khan (1271–1282), and Shamsuddin Firoz Shah (1301–1322). The latter achieved the Jihad of Sylhet and established a robust administration in eastern and southwestern Bengal. In 1325, the Delhi Sultan Ghiyath al-Din Tughluq reorganized the province into three administrative regions: Sonargaon Province in eastern Bengal, Gauda Province in northern Bengal, and Satgaon Province in southern Bengal.

The partition of Bengal didn't work as intended. In 1338, the three administrative regions had self-declared Sultans, including Fakhruddin Mubarak Shah in Sonargaon, Alauddin Ali Shah in Gauda, and Shamsuddin Ilyas Shah in Satgaon.

Fakhruddin declared Jihad against Chittagong's Buddhist petty tribal rulers in 1340 due to overwhelming complaints against these chieftains for systematically harassing Muslims in Chittagong. Ikhtiyaruddin Ghazi Shah, son of Fakruddin, earned the title "Ghazi" from the Delhi government and the Muslim masses for his victory in 1349, the highest honorable title for a living Mujahid. Shamsuddin Ilyas Shah (or Ilyas Shah) defeated Alauddin Ali Shah and secured control of Gauda. He then defeated Ikhtiyaruddin of Sonargaon. By 1352, Ilyas Shah emerged victorious among the Bengali rebellious self-declared rulers.

As we briefly review the history of Bengal, we learn that Hindu upper castes and Buddhist tribal chieftains systematically harassed Muslims in Bengal. Early Muslims in Bengal always faced problems with Hindus and Buddhists based on cultural and social differences. The fundamental issues revolved around practices like cow sacrificing, handshaking, and defecating in the paddy fields. Defecating in the paddy fields was a significant concern for Muslims, known as "Nizasa."

Early Muslims in Bengal lived within Hindu communities; their grandfathers or great-grandfathers migrated to Bengal for trade or to spread Islam. They purchased land from Hindu petty kings, settled, and built mosques and Islamic schools within the community. The new influx of Muslims came to fight against these petty Hindu kings and declared themselves rulers. In contrast, early Muslims lived within Hindu and Buddhist communities. The most significant psychological difference in Bengal over the last thousand years is that early Muslims sought to coexist peacefully with Hindus, Buddhists, and Christians, while newcomers aimed to exclude all non-Muslims from Bengal.

Shia Rule

Shia rule in Bengal was a confusing time for Muslims in Bengal after the Muslim victory in Bengal in 1202. Persians were migrating to Bengal, and the Persian language started influencing the Bengali Muslim language, leading to changes in formerly used Arabic words like "sawm" to "Roza" and "Salah" to "Namaz." Farsi replaced many other Arabic words.

In the twelfth century, Persians were welcomed into the Muslim Sultanate in Bengal for two specific reasons:

1. They brought with them millennia of military experience from the Persian Empire, which was valuable for military training in Bengal.
2. Their lighter skin color contrasted with the indigenous dark-skinned Bengalis.

These were the two main reasons Persians were allowed to settle in Muslim Bengal.

In 644, according to later accounts, Omar (Radeyallāhu 'Anhu) was assassinated by a Persian named Abu Lulu. The motivation for the assassination remains unclear to this day, with Islamic historians and scholars of Aqidah still disputing this matter. As history shows, Muslims divided into two groups right after Khalifa Umar's (Radeyallāhu 'Anhu) assassination.

One widespread interpretation is that the assassination was a response to the Muslim victory over the Persian Empire. Another conspiracy theory suggests that some Sunni Muslims believe Shi'ism originated from Persia as a Jewish conspiracy because the theological father of Shi'ism, ʿAbdullah ibn Sabaʾ al-Ḥimyarī, was a Jewish Rabbi.

However, scholars of Aqidah in Islam generally believe that Shia originated from a converted Jew, Rabbi ʿAbdullah ibn Sabaʾ al-Ḥimyarī. Political science scholars argue that Shiism began as a political faction rather than a religious sect, as evidenced by Umar's (Radeyallāhu 'Anhu) assassination.

In Bengal, some Sunnis believed that the Persians aimed to spread Shiism in Bengal, which was a hardcore Sunni stronghold. However, the Persians did not come to Bengal for religious preaching or trade. Arabs were primarily welcomed as Islamic religious preachers and traders, known for their honesty in business transactions and Islamic knowledge. There is no evidence of Persian dominance in religious education in Bengal, though Persian literature was widespread.

Before studying the differences between Shia and Sunni, I had little knowledge of this distinction. One day, I prayed Maghrib in a Shia Masjid in Jamaica, Queens, NY. My brother told me that it was a Shia Masjid. I asked him, "What's the difference between

Shia and Sunni?" He replied, "I don't know, but they pray differently than us." I noticed that, too. Afterward, I studied under prestigious Islamic scholars to understand the differences in Aqidah (creed). The number one authentic scholar in Islam said about Shia, referring to an authentic Hadith: "He who innovates something in this matter of ours (i.e., Islam) that is not of it will have it rejected by Allah." [Bukhari & Muslim]

Historians argue that the Persian resident Piruz Nahavandi (Abu Lulu) complained to Umar (Radeyallāhu 'Anhu) about the high tax imposed by his local ruler, Mughirah. Umar (Radeyallāhu 'Anhu) wrote to Mughirah, who responded satisfactorily, but Umar (Radeyallāhu 'Anhu) informed Abu Lulu that the tax was reasonable based on his income. Umar (Radeyallāhu 'Anhu) also requested that Abu Lulu make a windmill for him. In a sullen mood, Piruz said, "Verily, I will make such a mill for you that the whole world will remember it."

The hearsay is that some Jewish merchants assigned Piruz to assassinate Umar (Radeyallāhu 'Anhu). Just before the Fajr prayers, Piruz would enter Al-Masjid al-Nabawi, where Umar (Radeyallāhu 'Anhu) led the prayers, and would attack Umar (Radeyallāhu 'Anhu) during the prayers, then flee or blend with the congregation at the mosque.

On October 31, 644, Piruz attacked Umar (Radeyallāhu

'Anhu) during the morning prayers in the Masjid. He stabbed Umar six times in the belly and on the navel, causing a severe injury. Umar (Radeyallāhu 'Anhu) was bleeding as people tried to catch Piruz, who eventually committed suicide and injured about nine people in the mosque. He died before slashing himself with his blade to commit suicide, leaving his motive in suspense.

It's important to mention that in Islam, if someone is killed, they are considered martyrs. Some Islamic scholars hold the view that Umar (Radeyallāhu 'Anhu) always aspired to be a martyr after reverting to Islam. As a Khalifa, he couldn't participate on the battlefield, but Allah accepted him as a martyr.

Sarfarāz Khān was widely accused of spreading Shiism in Bengal, leading Sunni Muslims to boycott him. The Sunni upper-middle class (Mirasdar/Malik) tradition used to send their sons to join the military to defend Muslim states, but this practice ceased under Sarfarāz Khān. As a result, he heavily relied on the Hindu Kshatriya caste and made them Zamindars.

East India Company Rules

The rule of the East India Company in India is highly controversial among Indian freedom fighters, Hindu nationalists, Muslims in Bengal, and ordinary Indians. Most ordinary Indians appreciate the Company's rule in Bengal and India. In discussions at my college cafeteria with regular Indian students, they defended the Company and the British Government's rule in India. They argued that India would have remained stuck in a thousand-year-old caste system without the East India Company's rule in Bengal. Otherwise, they believed India might have been in a situation similar to undeveloped African countries. Furthermore, they pointed out that significant technological, bureaucratic, judicial, postal, telegraph and railroad developments might have yet to occur in India.

It's important to note that most Indians often mistakenly conflate the rule of the East India Company with British Rule. In reality, the East India Company was a mega-corporation founded in London in 1600. To understand India's internal conflicts, the Company created a policy to support small, local kings politically and financially, using money and military logistics, often with irrevocable treaties. Fundamentally, the East India Company was engaged in unconventional banking and unregulated interstate trading.

Historically, the East India Company first arrived in India in

1612. King James I sent Sir Thomas Roe to visit the Mughal Emperor Nur-ud-din Salim Jahangir (r. 1605–1627) to negotiate a trade treaty that would grant the Company exclusive rights to reside and establish businesses in Surat and other areas. In return, the Company offered to provide the Emperor with European goods and rarities. King James's expectations were met, and Emperor Jahangir sent a letter to King James through Sir Thomas Roe:

"Upon the assurance of your royal love, I have given my general command to all the kingdoms and ports of my dominions to receive all the merchants of the English nation as the subjects of my friend; that in whatever place they choose to live, they may have free liberty without any restraint. At whatever port they shall arrive, neither Portugal nor any other shall dare to molest their peace. In whatever city they reside, I have commanded all my governors and captains to grant them the freedom to buy, sell, and transport goods to their country at their pleasure. For confirmation of our love and friendship, I request Your Majesty to command your merchants to bring in their ships all sorts of rarities and rich goods fit for my palace. Please send me your royal letters by every opportunity, that I may rejoice in your health and prosperous affairs. May our friendship be eternal." (RCT)

Emperor Nur-ud-din Salim Jahangir was generous with Thomas Roe because of the Quranic verse referring to "Ahl al-kitābto" (people of the book). Ahl al-kitāb includes Jews, Christians,

Sabians, and, according to Islam, monotheistic people recognized as part of the Abrahamic religions. Hindus, considered polytheistic, were not included in this category.

However, the East India Company gradually increased its influence over the port cities in the Indian subcontinent, including Bengal.

The Battle of Plassey

The Battle of Plassey is widely known in the Indian subcontinent and by the British. Hundreds of books have been written, and movies have been made about this war. The story of Plassey is a complex political situation to explain briefly. I will touch on the core of it. The East India Company realized that the central government of Delhi was in a deep internal political crisis. The Company created a strategy to use petty kings against each other by promising military training, financial assistance with a low-interest rate loan, and a reasonable trade deal.

Lord Clive was a brilliant, sharp-minded military officer. He recognized that India had a rigid caste system, with Muslims as an insignificant minority but a ruling class. Additionally, Muslims were divided into two groups, Shia and Sunni, and the Sunnis would not support a Shia government. Moreover, Muhammad Siraj-ud-Daulah did not have a good relationship with the central government. This fearlessly led him to create a conspiracy to buy out Siraj-ud-Daulah's generals, which he successfully achieved. Without shedding blood, he easily won the war.

Lord Clive calculated the entire geopolitical crisis quite well. His victory in the Battle of Plassey was the most significant achievement for the British Government in hundreds of years. His political calculations changed the subcontinental political history, opening the path to eventual British rule.

Historically, after Siraj-ud-Daulah's success in Calcutta, the East India Company sent new troops from Madras to retake the fort and seek revenge for the attack. This led to the battle at Plassey, where Siraj-ud-Daulah established military camps approximately twenty-five miles away from Murshidabad.

On June 23, 1757, Siraj-ud-Daulah consulted with Mir Jafar due to the sudden death of Mir Mardan, a trusted general. The Nawab sought advice from Mir Jafar, who advised him to retreat for that day. Following his command, the Nawab's soldiers began returning to their camps. This was a strategic mistake on the battlefield, as stopping the fight without a ceasefire agreement or a decisive victory is against war strategy.

At the same time, Robert Clive seized the opportunity and attacked the Nawab's soldiers. He took full advantage of the unilateral ceasefire, a situation any army general would exploit, indicating the enemy's weakness and the opportunity for a decisive victory.

Before the war began, Lord Clive, Jagat Seth, Mir Jafar, Krishna Chandra, and Omichund had a roundtable meeting to orchestrate Nawab's defeat at Plassey. This defeat was well-planned by Lord Clive, Jagat Seth, Mir Jafar, Krishna Chandra, and Omichund.

As the Nawab's army headed to the camps for rest due to his orders, and it was challenging to reorder the soldiers for a counterattack, all fled from the battlefield, and Lord Clive easily won.

Mir Jafar's betrayal in Plassey led to the Nawab's defeat, and he fled to avoid arrest. He first went to Murshidabad, specifically to Hirajheel, his palace at Mansurganj. He ordered his senior commanders to bring their troops for his safety, but they refused to obey his order after his defeat at Plassey and supported him in defending the palace. Some advised him to surrender to the Company, and Nawab realized that it was a well-planned betrayal.

A few loyal commanders recommended encouraging the army with greater rewards, which he seemed to approve of, but it was too late. By then, the entire chain of command had collapsed.

On July 2, 1757, Siraj-ud-Daulah was executed by Mohammad Ali Beg under Mir Miran's order, the son of Mir Jafar, at Namak Haram Deorhi, as part of an agreement between Mir Jafar and the British East India Company to eliminate Siraj-ud-Daulah. This marked the end of the independence of what was referred to as Muslim Bongo (Bengal).

Hindu Zamindars

The rise of Hindu Zamindars in Bengal changed the entire culture of Bengal between 1793 and 1858. Historically, the defeat at Plassey was a total shock for Sunni Muslims in East Bengal. Muslims were confident that the Nawab would win the war easily because he had generous Hindu support, or Delhi would come to help him retake Bengal. However, the defeat was not good news for Muslims in India. The East India Company had become a de facto ruler, much like Mir Jafar's rule.

In 1793, the East India Company established a robust Hindu Zamindari system using European-style feudalism by forcibly taking land from Muslim Maliks/Mirasdars and leasing that land to newly-formed Hindu Zamindars/Rajas, known as the Permanent Settlement Act. They leased the land to these autonomous Rajas/Zamindars for ninety-nine years. The Company's strategy was to provide low-interest loans to these Hindu Rajas/Zamindars to build houses for operating the Zamindari.

The Company auctioned Muslim land to the Zamindars, limiting it to only two Hindu upper-caste groups, the Kshatriya and Brahmin castes, who pledged allegiance to the East India Company. Historically, the Shia rulers introduced the Zamindari system in Bengal. "Zamin" is a Farsi word for land, and "dar" is an Arabic word for home. Zamindar means Landlord (Estate). The East India

Company, originating from Europe, was well-versed in how feudalism worked, and they cleverly implemented European-style feudalism in India.

The rise of Hindu Zamindars during the East India Company rule led to a vicious cycle of socially discriminatory culture in Bengal. Hindu Zamindars often mistreated poor Muslims in Bengal, believing that the Sudras caste had converted to Islam to gain social status. They also banned Masjids and Islamic education. In Hinduism, Sudras were considered the lowest caste.

Some of my Hindu friends argue that Muslims also have a caste system. In the Muslim community, it is not a caste system but more of a social hierarchy. This system neither encourages nor discourages Islam. In the Quran, Allah said, "Say: 'O Allah! Possessor of the power, You give power to whom You will, and You take power from whom You will, and You endue with honor whom You will, and You humiliate whom You will. In Your Hand is good. Verily, You are able to do all things.'" (interpretation of the meaning) 3:26.

Respecting those with noble lineage is a Sunnah (tradition) and not an obligation, as it is in the core religious belief of Hinduism. Most noble-lineage Muslims are humble toward Allah, but being born into a noble-lineage family does not necessarily equate to an easy lifestyle, as some people may assume. Maintaining humility often requires controlling ego, arrogance, and pride.

Some Maliks compromised with the Company to obtain the Zamindari title to protect their assets from East India Company seizures, but my great-grandfather never compromised. Our Mirasdari remained an independent Mirasdari until the East Pakistan government dissolved it in 1950 under the Land Reform Act.

The Zamindari system did not benefit either Muslims or Hindus in Bengal. It only served to help the East India Company and the British Government accumulate wealth for the UK. Muslims in Bengal became increasingly impoverished due to high taxes and high-interest rates imposed by the East India Company and the British Government through the Zamindari system.

British Rule

The British Rule, known as the British Raj, signifies British governance over the Indian subcontinent from 1858 to 1947. It spanned almost a century, during which the British provinces of the Indian subcontinent were partitioned into two countries, India and Pakistan, while the British princely states were given the choice to align with one of these new nations.

The British Raj was characterized by the British Crown's rule over the Indian subcontinent from 1858 to 1947, with local rulers pledging allegiance to the British Crown instead of Delhi. The British Government held responsibility for defense, foreign policy, and the economy. A Royal Crown judicial system was introduced to ensure justice according to the decrees of the British Empire. Because the British Raj fell under British Crown jurisdiction, it was often referred to as British India.

This system of governance was established on June 28, 1858, when, following the Indian Rebellion of 1857, the British East India Company transferred authority to Queen Victoria of the British Crown, who was proclaimed Empress of India in 1876.

Calcutta served as the capital of the British Raj from 1858 to 1911. However, due to communal social unrest between Muslims and Hindus in Bengal, the British Government decided to relocate the capital to Delhi.

On August 15, 1947, the British Raj was permanently dissolved, leading to the creation of two nations, India and Pakistan. Unfortunately, law and order collapsed in the newly formed Pakistan, resulting in tragic Hindu-Muslim riots and an unimaginable refugee crisis. This marked the end of British rule, a period that brought immense suffering to millions and left a wound that seemed impossible to heal.

Lord Curzon

Lord Curzon played a critical role for Muslims in Bengal. With the sharp rise of Hindu Zamindaris, tensions were escalating between Hindus and Muslims, and village-to-village quarrels were on the rise. Proza (possibly referring to a Muslim community or group) were strictly prohibited from wearing sandals. It became the daily duty of Mirasdars or Maliks to listen to the grievances of poor Muslims, who complained about harassment, torture, lynching, and systematic discriminatory abuses by Hindu Rajas or Zamindars based on religious affiliation, often for minor issues such as wearing sandals.

When Lord Curzon was appointed as Viceroy and Governor-General of India, he expressed his desire to meet with Muslim Nawabs, Mirasdars, and Maliks. Muslims, including my great-grandfather Muhammed Hasim Khalisdar, met with Lord Curzon. They voiced their concerns about the systematic humiliation of poor Muslims by Hindu Zamindars. Consequently, they expressed their desire for an independent Muslim country.

Lord Curzon denied the request for the creation of an independent nation, but he was willing to consider the partition of Bengal if they promised to engage in a political process and put an end to the violence. The Muslim leaders agreed to Lord Curzon's proposal.

Partition of Bengal

The partition of Bengal was not a new concept for Muslims, as they had previously united Bongo (Bengal) by toppling small, petty kings in 1200 AD. In 1325, Bongo (Bengal) was partitioned by the Muslim Sultanate in Delhi. Familiar with this historical precedent, Muslims did not object to the division of Bengal; instead, they agreed with Lord Curzon's proposal to partition Bengal.

On July 20, 1905, Lord Curzon announced the division of Bengal into East and West Bengal. Upon hearing of this partition, Bengali Proza Muslims held great admiration for Rabindranath Tagore, a scion of an East Bengal Zamindar family, who composed the song "Amar Sonar Bangla" on the same day.

It is essential to mention that the Tagore family once controlled one-third of the East Bengal estate (Zamindari). Their grand residence was located in Calcutta, West Bengal. The partition of Bengal was heart-wrenching for the Tagore family as they learned that East Bengal would be under Muslim rule.

Ironically, nearly thirty percent of East Bengalis were part of the Tagore family's proza, the very people who used to complain to Muslim Mirasdars, Nawabs, or Maliks about the Tagore family's systematic social humiliation and discrimination. Today, their descendants identify as proud Bengalis, and their love for their former masters is an emotionally charged sentiment.

The main reason for the partition of Bengal was the social discrimination practiced by Hindu Zamindars against Krishaks (farmers) and Praja (Proza) Muslims, a term that technically means enslaved people in Hindu scripture. Additionally, Hindu Zamindars obstructed Proza Muslims from obtaining British Government jobs and from attending Masjids, Madrassas, schools, and colleges.

The British Government jobs were categorized according to the Hindu caste system, consisting of four classes. The first-class job was typically allocated to the British, Hindu Kshatriyas, Brahmins, and Muslim upper-class individuals such as Mirasdars, Maliks, or Nawabs. Kshatriyas and a few Muslims dominated the second-class job. Hindu Vaishyas were prominent in the third-class job, with limited Muslim representation. However, supervisory or managerial positions in the third-class job were reserved for the British. The fourth-class job was primarily for Hindu Sudras, with Muslims occasionally occupying supervisory roles.

Nevertheless, the authorities of the British Raj initiated a territorial reorganization of the Bengal Presidency, as promised by Lord Curzon. This act was implemented on October 16, 1905. On December 30, 1906, the Muslim League was formed, with my grandfather, Muhammed Massim Khalisdar, representing the State of Assam in support of the Muslim League's formation as a political party in compliance with the British legal framework aimed at serving the interests of India's Muslims.

Bengali Wins Freedom

From 1772 to 1858, all Zamindari certifications, known as Deeds or Dalils, were exclusively issued to Hindus by the East India Company. This led to the accumulation of substantial wealth among Hindus in Bengal over the course of a century. They gained significant political and economic influence over British decisions in India. These influential Hindus lobbied British lawmakers in London to reunite Bengal. Their primary concern was that Muslims might revert to the Malik system, signifying land ownership under Islamic Law (Sharia). This system allowed individuals to own land through inheritance, purchase, or as a gift, and if a piece of land remained unused for 3-5 years, a homeless Muslim could claim it for shelter. Muslims paid Zakat, Nisab, and sometimes taxes to the Muslim Government for efficient state governance, which concerned Hindu Zamindars in contrast to British land ownership laws.

Under strong lobbying from Hindu influencers, Lord Hardinge decided to reunite Bengal. This decision was intended to appease the sentiments of Hindu Zamindars and business owners. The Hindu oligarchy successfully convinced the British establishment in London that Muslims would implement Sharia law, replacing Crown rules. They accused Muslims of looting Hindu properties, raping Hindu women, and defiling Hindu houses with cow meat, while Hindus revered cows as sacred animals. Hindu women were taken as Khadima by Muslims. Implementing Islamic

Law in Bengal, they argued, would lead to the collapse of the British Indian economy in Bengal.

Following a royal decree by King George in December 1911, Eastern Bengal was amalgamated into the Bengal Presidency without British Parliamentary hearings, as it was deemed necessary to defuse the violence in Bengal. This decision marked a turning point for Muslim politics in Bengal. Muslims in Bengal viewed it as a breach of trust and began their journey towards the creation of a Muslim nation.

Bengali Nationalism

On April 14, 2004, a BBC opinion poll named Sheikh Mujibur Rahman the greatest Bengali of all time. I wonder why Sheikh Mujibur Rahman holds this title. It became clear to me that it is because, using him as their leader, the Bengalis liberated themselves from the process of Muslimization during the period of Pakistan in Bengal.

Historically, the Bengali Nationalist movement, known as the Bengali Renaissance, was initiated by the Tagore family. Rabindranath Tagore and Dwarkanath Tagore, prominent leaders of this period, envisioned educational reforms in the Bengali language and sought to make Bengali the official language of the Bengal province. Other notable members of this Hindu family, such as Gaganendranath, Jyotirindranath, Abanindranath, Jyotirindranath Tagore, Asit Kumar Haldar, and Jnanadanandini Devi, were also associated with the movement.

After the 1857 Mutiny, the British Government endorsed the academic introduction of regional languages as a second official language in the British Raj and British Indian provinces. This greatly favored Bengali literature. Pioneers like Ram Mohan Roy and Iswar Chandra Vidyasagar were joined by others, including Bankim Chandra Chatterjee, Pramatha Chaudhuri, Upendrakishore Roy Chowdhury, and Dwarkanath Ganguly, who expanded the movement and established a solid intellectual foundation.

In contrast, Sheikh Mujibur Rahman's political career began in the late 1940s as a street picketer for the Muslim League and later as a tea-boy in Huseyn Shaheed Suhrawardy's office.

The Tagore family, being one of the largest Hindu Zamindars in East Bengal, was directly connected with King George. This connection allowed them to champion the Bengali movement effectively.

While Bangladeshi Bengalis highly admire Sheikh Mujibur Rahman as a Bengali leader and savior, and he holds the title of the greatest Bengali, his historical and political contributions to the Bengali movement are rather limited.

The beginning of the East Bengali nationalist movement can be traced back to March 21, 1948, when the Governor-General of Pakistan, Mohammad Ali Jinnah, addressed a large crowd at the Dhaka Race Course Field. His speech seemed dictatorial, as he accused enemies and conspirators against Pakistan rather than seeking unity for the new nation. Jinnah declared that "Urdu and Urdu alone" would be Pakistan's official language, even though Bengalis constituted the majority in the new country.

Linguistic tensions between Urdu and Bengali were further exacerbated by Governor-General Khawaja Nazimuddin, who staunchly defended the "Urdu-only" policy in a speech on January

27, 1952.

On January 31, 1952, the Shorbodolio Kendrio Rashtrabhasha Kormi Porishod (All-Party Central Language Action Committee) was formed at the Bar Library Hall meeting at Dhaka University, chaired by Maulana Bhashani. During the meeting, the idea of writing Bengali in Arabic script was proposed but was not accepted by the committee.

The action committee called for a comprehensive protest on February 21, demanding that Bengali be recognized as Pakistan's official language. This protest included strikes and rallies across East Bengal. Chief Minister Nurul Amin imposed Section 144 in Dhaka to prevent the demonstration, thereby banning any gatherings.

On 7 May 1954, the Constituent Assembly voted in support of Bengali as one of the official languages of Pakistan. Two years later, on 21 February 1956, the National Assembly of Pakistan declared both Urdu and Bengali the official state languages of Pakistan.

Understanding the historical language issue in Bengal requires considering that, apart from Traditional Muslim families, it may be challenging to comprehend why most Muslim Leaguers advocated for Urdu as an official language. Even prominent political leaders like Maulana Bhashani endorsed the use of Arabic script instead of Bengali.

Historically, Muslims migrated to Bengal from Khaleej, Yemen trade and spread Islam, and later, Turks and Persians. At that time, there was no unified Bengal but instead a collection of small, local rulers known as Rajas. These Rajas had official Mandirs where preachers would recite mantras in Sanskrit. Arabic was the language spoken by Khaleeji and Yemani Muslims. When these migrants converted to Islam, they were taught Arabic, and Arabic words were incorporated into the local language, leading to the development of a new Muslim language in Bengal.

In the 14th century, Persians migrated to Bongo (Bengal), and the Farsi language gradually influenced the Bengali Muslim language. It led to the replacement of Arabic words, such as Sawm to Roza and Salah to Namaz, among others. The spread of Persian literature, stories, and poems further influenced Bengal.

The fear of Shiism spreading in Bengal due to the Persian influence created tension within the Sunni establishment. It is important to note that Khaleeji and Yemani Muslims were Sunni, and the Persians mixed with Sunni, Shia, and Zoroastrianism.

In the view of the Muslims in Bengal, Farsi was considered a Shia language, and Bengali was associated with Hindus, leaving them to create a new language, Urdu. Urdu was a mixture of Arabic and the local Indian language. After the creation of Pakistan, the push for Urdu as the official language disregarded the wishes of the majority.

Hindu intellectuals worked tirelessly to gain international recognition for the Bengali language. Nearly everyone in Bangladesh needs to understand and interpret the entire history of the language movement. The proposal to make Urdu Pakistan's official language wounded the egos of Hindu elites and intensified their jealousy. Therefore, orchestrating the Bengali language movement became necessary for them.

While many believe that the Bengali language movement was aimed at dismembering United Pakistan, I must respectfully disagree with this argument. As the grandson of a Muslim League founding member and the son of a late Muslim League leader, I am confident that Jinnah was the root cause of Pakistan's internal and external issues. Jinnah was an opportunistic egotist and a puppet of the British Government rather than a true politician.

On February 21st, from 1969 to this day, Every year, East Bengalis celebrate Bhasha Diwas, also known as Mother Language Day, which is observed to encourage Begalis to feel proud of the Bengali Language.

Bengali Hindu Homeland

As Bangladeshi Bengalis mourn their Bengali nationalistic identity every night and day, and annually on February 21, they barefootedly lay flowers on the monuments. It seemed to me that they were unaware that their former leader, Mukherjee, desired a Bengali Hindu Homeland.

I'd like to briefly discuss the Bengali Hindu Homeland Movement. Syama Prasad Mukherjee was a prominent leader of this movement among Bengali Hindus. He joined the Hindu Mahasabha in Bengal in 1939 and became its acting president the same year. In 1940, he was appointed as the working president of the organization.

In February 1941, Mukherjee delivered a speech at a Hindu rally, suggesting that if Muslims wished to live in Pakistan, they should "pack their bags and baggage and leave India... [to] wherever they like." He was elected as the President of Akhil Bharatiya Hindu Mahasabha in 1943. However, while Mukherjee served as the organization's working president, the Hindu Mahasabha formed provincial coalition governments with the All-India Muslim League in Sindh and the North-West Frontier Province. In the same year, Laxman Bhopatkar assumed the role of the organization's new president.

Mukherjee called for the partition of Bengal in 1946 to prevent an inclusive Hindu-Muslim Bengal. He expressed concerns that the Hindu minority in a Muslim-dominated East Pakistan, or Bengalistan, would face significant challenges.

On April 15, 1947, in Tarakeswar, the Mahasabha held a meeting authorizing Syama Prasad Mukherjee to advocate for Bengal's partition along religious lines.

An unsuccessful attempt for a united, independent Bengal was made by Sarat Bose, the brother of Subhas Chandra Bose, and Huseyn Shaheed Suhrawardy, a Muslim League leader.

In May 1947, Syama Prasad Mukherjee wrote a letter to Lord Mountbatten, stating that Bengal must be partitioned, even if India remained a Union. He also opposed the idea of a united, independent Bengal in 1947, citing the Noakhali Hindu genocide in East Bengal, where Muslim mobs massacred Hindus and looted their properties.

It was Mukherjee who spearheaded the Bengali Hindu Homeland Movement. This movement involved Bengali Hindu people advocating for the partition of Bengal in 1947 to create a homeland in West Bengal for themselves within the Indian Union. This was in response to the Muslim League's proposal and campaign to include the entire province of Bengal within Pakistan.

Muslim League

In bedtime stories, I heard from my Boro Ma (culturally, we call Boro Ma to a woman who comes to the family as the first wife of uncles or father's cousins) that my grandfather took a horse to Dhaka to participate in the Muslim League meeting. Dhaka Nawab sent a risalah (official invitation) to my great-grandfather, Muhammed Hasim Khalisdar, but he refused to go to Dhaka due to his health concerns. Instead, my grandfather, Muhammed Masim Khalisdar, went as one of the Assam state delegates in winter.

My grandfather attended the meeting not because he agreed with creating a political party. He went to the summit only because my great-grandfather had promised Lord Curzon that he would be part of a political process if Bengal were to be partitioned. The Prophet (peace and blessings of Allaah be upon him) said: "There are four characteristics; whoever has them is a hypocrite, and whoever has one of the four has a characteristic of hypocrisy unless he gives it up: when he speaks, he lies; when he makes a promise, he breaks it; when he makes a pledge, he betrays it; and when he disputes, he resorts to foul language." (al-Bukhaari, 2327; Muslim, 58).

On December 30, 1906, the Muslim League was officially formed. Its objective was to educate Muslims in mathematics, English, Science, and the Quran, integrating them with the British

Government. This aimed to encourage Muslims to take on governmental jobs, as many Muslims used to avoid the British due to derogatory labels such as "Bania" or the threat of guerrilla attacks.

This period marked the first time in Muslim history when Muslims organized politically to advance their interests in Bengal and Assam. The Muslim League also laid the foundation for uniting Muslims in India.

Despite opposition from some quarters, including a fatwa issued by a cleric against learning English, the Muslim League encouraged its members to teach their children English to compete with Hindus.

During a lunch break, some Muslim Leaguers asked the Dhaka Nawab to build a university in Dhaka. The Nawab responded humorously, "We've just formed a new province and a new party. Can't we wait a few more years?" Everyone shared a laugh in the hall.

However, the Muslim League found itself largely confined within the Muslim bourgeoisie and struggled to reach ordinary Muslims. To address this, they decided to employ Maulana Bhashani, internationally known as the Red Maulana, to work with impoverished Muslims in support of the Muslim League agenda. Despite initial skepticism about Maulana Bhashani's commitment to the Muslim League's objectives, he played a pivotal role in bringing the Muslim League into the limelight, particularly in Assam and Bengal.

On August 16, 1946, the Muslim League declared a day of nationwide protest led by Jinnah, leading to large-scale violence between Muslims and Hindus in Calcutta, within the Bengal province of British India.

This incident has an interesting backstory. Bangladeshi Bengali Father Sheikh Mujibur Rahman narrated the story to East Bengal Muslim League leaders after creating the Awami Muslim League: "We three made Pakistan, "Jinnah, Huseyn Shaheed Suhrawardy, and I. So don't question our patriotism."

According to the Mujib's claim, Jinnah telegraphed Huseyn Shaheed Suhrawardy, Chief Minister of Bengal, regarding the British government's intention to change the Governor-General. Under the new administration, it would take more work to make a case for Pakistan. In response, Chief Minister Suhrawardy communicated under British Governmental confidentiality rules that "all the options are on the table except the partition of Bengal." This was a signal for the Calcutta riot.

After the telegraph, Huseyn Shaheed Suhrawardy asked Mujib in his office, "Khoka, can you take care of Calcutta?" Mujib replied, "Jee, Sir." It's worth noting that Mujib was very close to Huseyn Shaheed Suhrawardy. In the 1946 election, Mujib served as

Huseyn Shaheed Suhrawardy's right-hand man. The Bengal Provincial Muslim League won the 1946 general election, receiving the largest number of Assembly seats in Bengal, which was interpreted as a referendum for Pakistan. The nature of Mujib's close relationship with Huseyn Shaheed Suhrawardy remains a mystery.

During the riots in the late 1940s, a friend named Shen came to my father's house in Howrah, India. Shen was my father's college friend. He urged my father to get into his jeep quickly, saying, "I will take you close to Benapole." When my father asked why, Shen explained, "The Butcher of Calcutta, the Khoka gang, is mercilessly killing Hindus and looting Hindu stores. In retaliation, Hindu mobs are killing Muslims and looting Muslim property. I heard you are a target because you were a Muslim student activist in college. They are coming after you. You have two choices: stay and die or go with me to save your life. I can't wait too long; they will kill me too."

My father got into Shen's jeep with a few of his other friends, tears in his eyes as he left the house that had been built by his great-great-grandfather a hundred years ago. He was leaving it in the hands of the mobs. Shen dropped him off at Benapole, giving him a pack of cigarettes and a hug. My father said, "It was not expected." Shen replied, "It was expected when Suhrawardy was elected as Chief Minister." His right-hand man, "Khoka," was a well-known goon.

In the late 1940s, two major political parties, the Muslim League and the Indian National Congress, were the largest political entities in British India. The Muslim League had been demanding the creation of Pakistan since the 1940 Lahore Resolution, advocating for Muslim-majority areas in the Northwest and the East to form Pakistan.

In 1946, the British India Cabinet Mission discussed three possibilities for the political structure: a center, groups of provinces, and individual provinces. The "groups of provinces" concept was intended to accommodate the Muslim League's demand. In principle, both the Muslim League and Congress accepted the Cabinet Mission's plan. However, the Muslim League suspected that Congress's acceptance was a political-strategic move rather than a genuine commitment.

After extensive discussions among key figures such as Huseyn Shaheed Suhrawardy, Abul Kasem Fazlul Huq, Khwaja Nazimuddin, Abdus Sabur Khan, Nurul Amin, and Kazi Qader, among others, the meeting heavily debated the "three-states theory." Finally, the Muslim League decided that they were Muslim brothers who must remain united as one nation. Additionally, they recognized that Banglastan, if separated, would exist as a minority within a larger non-Muslim country, which would pose significant challenges. Therefore, the Muslim League resolved to fight for the two-nation theory.

In July 1946, the Muslim League withdrew from the three-states theory agreement with the British Government. Jinnah announced a general strike (hartal) on August 16, known as Direct Action Day, to assert its demand for a separate homeland for Indian Muslims in specific Northwestern and Eastern provinces of British India.

Huseyn Shaheed Suhrawardy's right-hand man, Khoka, orchestrated a violent communal riot during a closed-door meeting. The protest resulted in widespread bloodshed and looting in Calcutta, with more than 4,000 innocent lives lost and 100,000 residents left homeless in Calcutta within just three days. These riots subsequently spread to Noakhali, Bihar, the United Provinces, Punjab, and the Northwestern Frontier Province. The depth of religious hatred was so profound that no leader knew how to control it.

On August 14, 1947, Pakistan was born under the leadership of the Muslim League. In a closed-door meeting, Louis Francis Albert Victor Nicholas Mountbatten and Jinnah conspired to make Karachi the capital of Pakistan and transferred power to Jinnah, declaring him the Governor-General of Pakistan with the British Crown as the Head of the State. Mountbatten's justification was that Dhaka was too far from Bombay or Delhi, and Pakistan could sort things out after the transfer of power.

In 1948, the Muslim League split into two groups. The Muslim League Jinnah group adhered to the core principles of secularism and allegiance to the British Crown. The British Crown was regarded as the King of Pakistan, with Jinnah as the Governor-General. The Aga Khani Shia community dominated the Muslim League Jinnah faction. Meanwhile, the Pakistan Muslim League's core principle was the Islamic Republic of Pakistan, advocating for provincial autonomy, a divided Pakistan into East and West, and a central government representing the Islamic Republic of United Pakistan. The leadership structure included a Khalifa or President as the head of United Pakistan and the prime ministership. Members of the national assembly would elect the Prime Minister. Dhaka was intended to serve as the Parliamentarian Capital, while West Pakistan would have a Presidential or Khalifat capital.

In June 1949, the Muslim League faced a significant setback, marking the beginning of the end for the party. Abdul Hamid Khan Bhashani, who had been instrumental in advancing the Muslim League movement in Bengal and Assam, decided to create a new political party known as the Awami Muslim League, often referred to as the "Muslim League's Gandhi." Without Abdul Hamid Khan Bhashani's support, the Muslim League lost a critical pillar. Bhashani had been the heart and mind of the poor Muslim population in Bengal and Assam.

In 1950, the East Pakistan Estate Acquisition Act of 1950

had a significant impact on Hindu Zamindars and Muslim League leaders alike. The majority of Muslim leaders were landowners, and this law particularly affected Hindu landowners, who held more than 80% of the East Pakistan estate (Zamindari).

During the 1954 election in the East Bengal province of Pakistan, the Muslim League suffered a significant defeat. A united front comprising Socialists, Federalists, and Communists demonstrated their influence, effectively marking the end of the Muslim League's popularity. Despite this, my father managed to win his constituency.

In 1958, Ayub Khan took over the leadership. To the relief of many Muslim Leaguers, there was a sense of optimism. The Pakistan Muslim League did not protest Ayub Khan's takeover; instead, they welcomed it. In contrast, the Muslim League Jinnah group strongly opposed the military takeover. The era of President Ayub Khan seemed like a honeymoon period for the Pakistan Muslim League, but it ultimately ended in humiliation.

During the 1970 election, the Muslim League was virtually wiped out in both East and West Pakistan. The Pakistan Muslim League could not secure more than ten seats in United Pakistan. However, there were predictions that the Muslim League would win over a hundred seats, fueled by speculation of Indian conspiracies and ongoing violence. Muslim League voters were primarily in the age group between 40 and 60.

Nevertheless, the outcome of the 1970 election was influenced by various factors. After the 1970 cyclones in East Pakistan, the political landscape underwent a dramatic transformation. The pro-Mujib media capitalized on the cyclone, portraying it as Pakistani sabotage against East Pakistani Bengalis.

Following the East Pakistan Estate Acquisition Act of 1950, Hindu Zamindars, who lost billions of dollars in East Pakistan's assets, fueled discontent. Approximately fifteen thousand Hindu Raja and Zamindars, who owned more than 80% of the East Pakistan estate, lost their properties overnight, leading to widespread outrage.

Former Hindu Zamindars propagated rumors among their nearly fifty million former tenants (proza), claiming that Pakistanis intended to enslave Bengalis. These rumors escalated into intense animosity between Bengalis and Pakistanis, which ultimately contributed to the downfall of the Muslim League. Additionally, various political parties alleged that the election had been rigged by Yahya Khan, the Mujibur Rahman-led eight-party coalition, and Bhutto, marking the end of the Muslim League.

Sher E Bengal

As history suggests, the Muslim bourgeois class formed the Muslim League. There was a lack of representation of poor Muslims in the party. As far as I know, there was no biography of Abul Kasem Fazlul Huq; therefore, defining Abul Kasem Fazlul Huq's political agenda is challenging. I know for a fact that Abul Kasem Fazlul Huq was inspired by Karl Marx's political theory and worked relentlessly toward socialism. He strongly identified himself as a Muslim and was willing to collaborate with Muslim Leaguers. He was also the founder of the Krishak Praja Party.

His party had two main elements:

1. Krishak: Krishak referred to those who worked for Muslim Malik/Mirasdar as farmers. The land belonged to Malik/Mirasdar, and the Krishak worked as a farmer while the Mirasdar/Malik paid them.
2. Praja (Proza): According to the 1793 East India Company Act, the Proza/Praja were technically considered slaves to the Zamindars.

The 1793 Act of the East India Company intensified tensions between Muslim Malik/Mirasdar and Hindu Zamindars. In Islam, Muslims believe in brotherhood, and poor Muslims are considered as Fakir and Miskin, not enslaved individuals. Muslims referred to paid workers as "Kamla." An essential hadith known to all Muslim leaders states, "Pay the worker his dues before his sweat has dried up." Calling a free Muslim a slave angered the Muslim bourgeois class.

However, Abul Kasem Fazlul Huq was invited to participate in the Muslim League meeting. Before the official declaration of the Muslim League on December 30, in negotiations with some founding members of the Muslim Leaguers, Abul Kasem Fazlul Huq agreed to join the Muslim Movement, but he never abandoned his socialist agenda. For nearly three days, leading Muslim Nawabs and Mirasdar discussed the Muslim League agenda with Abul Kasem Fazlul Huq. The Muslim League had become a political representative for Muslims in British India.

In the 1930-32 Roundtable Conference in London, Abul Kasem Fazlul Huq unequivocally demanded a Muslim independent state in front of the King. At that very moment, he received the title from the famous Muslim poet Muhammad Iqbal and Dhaka Nawab "Sher E Bengal." In contrast, Jinnah was preoccupied with his 14 points for loose Indian federalism.

On March 23, 1940, at Minto Park in Lahore, the All India Muslim League, presented a two-nation theory delivered by Sher E Bengal A.K. Fazlul Huq. Behind the scenes, the so-called Working Committee had intense debates about India's partition based on Hindu and Muslim lines or Federal India. Jinnah repeatedly emphasized his 14 points, while leaders like Jawaharlal Nehru, Subhas Chandra Bose, and Vallabhbhai Jhaverbhai Patel sought a strong, Centralized United Union of India or one Indian policy. Jinnah enjoyed reliable support from Shia groups such as the Aga Khan, which allowed him some flexibility.

In a closed-door meeting, the Sunni group turned to A.K. Fazlul Huq, saying, "We trust your judgment. You have a wealth of political experience and knowledge in British and Islamic law. You must guide us in this challenging moment." A.K. Fazlul Huq responded with, "Today or never," and publicly presented the two-nation theory. This move surprised Jinnah and hurt his ego since he did not expect A.K. Fazlul Huq's two-nation theory to be declared openly.

The Shia group, led by the Aga Khan, was infuriated by A.K. Fazlul Huq's two-nation theory. Their viewpoint was straightforward: Muslims cannot govern a country, and the British Crown should be the Head of State.

If the Shia establishment had not distorted Pakistan's history, A.K. Fazlul Huq could have been recognized as the Father of Pakistan, and Pakistan might have been more stable and prosperous. A.K. Fazlul Huq's idea of uniting the three Pakistans into one, with East Pakistan and West Pakistan as two wings and the Federal Government representing the Islamic Republic of United Pakistan, could have been the right solution for Pakistan. The Federal Government would have jurisdiction over Foreign Policy, the Defense Ministry, the Finance Ministry, the Communication Ministry, and Regional Ministries.

Khwaja Nazimuddin

Khwaja Nazimuddin was born into a Nawab family. I disapprove of the Dhaka Nawab because Nawabs used to be appointed by the Delhi Sultanate. Historically, the Delhi Sultanate made administrative changes several times in the past, and the British Government abolished the last Mughal, Mirza Abu Zafar Siraj-ud-din Muhammad, on September 21, 1857. Therefore, the Dhaka Nawab was not a legitimate Muslim Nawab; the British appointed them. Sunni Muslims never accepted the British Government as the legitimate ruler of India.

However, Dhaka Nawab Nawab Sir Khwaja Salimullah Bahadur made significant contributions to Muslims in East Bengal. He worked tirelessly to unite Muslims in Dhaka and invested a substantial amount of money in Muslim interests. He also laid the foundation for Dhaka University.

In short, Khwaja Nazimuddin was not a sincere political leader like Khwaja Salimullah. He was much more ambitious than a politician. He aligned himself with Jinnah to make the British Crown the Head of the State and the Governor-General of United Pakistan. Both were obsessed with the British concept of Governor Generalship. However, he did agree with the name "Islamic Republic of Pakistan" under the British Crown.

Huseyn Shaheed Suhrawardy

Huseyn Shaheed Suhrawardy was not a founding member of the Muslim League and did not subscribe to the Muslim League's political strategy. In a sense, he was deeply rooted in his emotional connection to Islam. Throughout his entire political career, he exhibited a tendency to change his political ideological positions. His political ambitions grew after he met his right-hand man, Khoka, who is considered the father of the nation in Bangladesh. The Calcutta riot occurred under his watch and significantly influenced the debate in the British Parliament. Without Huseyn Shaheed Suhrawardy and Mujib, the birth of Pakistan would likely not have occurred.

From a political perspective, Suhrawardy envisioned a Federal Pakistan with provincial autonomy, which was in contrast to Jinnah's vision. He believed in regional autonomy and advocated for limiting federal government interference in local internal political matters. He expressed the view that "Pakistan should be recognized as an independent nation, free from the authority of the British Crown."

Chapter Three

Jinnah

Muhammad Ali Jinnah is widely respected in Pakistan (West Pakistan 1955-1971). I have never been fond of Jinnah. I was inspired by Boro Ma's bedtime stories about my grandfather's Muslim League political activism at an early age. Secondly, I was inspired by Prophet Muhammed's (PBUH) biography book (I forgot the exact name).

In the winter of 1906, my grandfather rode on horseback from Rajapur, Sylhet, to Dhaka to participate in the Muslim League's formation. His efforts to engage Muslim Mirasdars, Zamindars, and Maliks in discussions about the Muslim League's progress at our Tongi (bungalow) or his travels to Calcutta were stories that deeply resonated with me.

I only heard a little about Jinnah during my childhood. I recall hearing about him a few times, particularly during my father's coffee table discussions in Sylhet, where my father would spontaneously refer to him as "Ekta Gaddaar," signifying that Jinnah had no respect within our family. Jinnah was scarcely a topic of discussion in Bangladeshi Muslim family gatherings.

However, my understanding of Jinnah grew through my exposure to various mediums like listening, reading, discussing, and watching YouTube. I perceive him as not being as dedicated or sincere as leaders like George Washington or Nelson Mandela, but rather an opportunist waiting for the right chance to seize an opportunity.

Jinnah's father, Jinnahbhai Poonja, aspired for his son to emulate the English. He exerted great effort to ensure Jinnah became a barrister. There was nothing particularly remarkable about Jinnah, apart from his relentless pursuit of a better life, much like any parent striving to provide a better future for their children.

During his time as a student in London, Jinnah's curiosity and ambition led him to meet Dadabhai Naoroji, through whom he became involved in British politics. Dadabhai Naoroji, the first Asian to become a British MP, served as Jinnah's inspiration, boosting his confidence in British political circles.

According to the history of the Indian Congress Party, Jinnah expressed his political ambitions by attending the Congress's twentieth annual meeting in Bombay in December 1904. He established his Indian nationalism on the principle of secularism, aligning himself with figures like Mehta, Naoroji Gopal, and Krishna Gokhale. He was recognized as a moderate Muslim youth.

In the late 1930s, Jinnah sought to join the Muslim League, which was met with challenges from its members. He claimed that Mohammed Iqbal wanted him to join the League. Jinnah found support from the Aga Khani Shia group within the Muslim League despite significant political differences. Jinnah envisioned a weak Federal India with the British Crown as its head, while Congress leaders advocated for a centralized, united India, and the Muslim League pushed for an independent Muslim country.

The contrasts were stark. Jinnah's father, Jinnahbhai Poonja, instilled in him a belief in the superiority of the English over Indians and Muslims, leaving him unable to think outside this framework, lacking historical knowledge, wisdom, and political acumen to resolve issues, and firmly convinced of the backwardness of Muslims and Indians.

The Sunni upper and middle classes in Bengal fought against British occupation to achieve an independent Muslim country, highlighting the stark psychological differences between Jinnah and the Sunni Muslim League founding members. While the latter fought against British rule, Jinnah remained submissive to British superiority.

Jinnah faced widespread accusations of being a British agent in Bengal. Nonetheless, in 1947, through a closed-door deal with Lord Mountbatten, he managed to secure Karachi as the capital with himself as the Governor-General. His fixation on the title "Governor-General" was palpable.

In the first week of August 1947, senior Muslim League

leaders in Dhaka anticipated the arrival of Lord Mountbatten, only to receive a telegram announcing Jinnah and Lord Mountbatten's agreement to establish Pakistan. This act was seen as a breach of trust, deeply dishonorable to the Muslim martyrs in Bengal who had sacrificed their lives with the hope of liberating Bengal from British rule. Jinnah would forever remain in the hearts and minds of Bengalis as a traitorous opportunist.

Pakistan

The historical account of the Creation of Pakistan needs to be clarified. As the grandson of a Muslim League founding member, I can see through these falsehoods. I aim to provide an accurate chronicle of the historical events that led to Pakistan's formation.

On June 23, 1757, under the leadership of Major-General Robert Clive, the first British victory in South Asia took place. This battle enabled the British East India Company to establish control over independent Bengal. The coalition government of Shia and Hindus crumbled, as the Sunni establishment had anticipated Delhi's support in regaining Bengal from Mir, Jafar, and Lord Clive, but it never materialized. On September 21, 1857, the Sunni Muslim government was dissolved and replaced by the British Crown.

The Permanent Settlement Act of May 1, 1793, established Hindu Raja and Zamindars as autonomous rulers in Bengal villages. This led to the systematic mistreatment, humiliation, and lynching of poor Muslims by Hindu Zamindars a new sparking tension and mistrust between the two communities.

My great-grandfather, Muhammed Hasim, tried to resolve these issues by meeting with Raja Girish Chandra Roy. However, the promises made during these meetings turned out to be empty, deepening the divide. The Permanent Settlement Act had given Hindu Rajas and Zamindars a sense of perpetual power under the protection of the East India Company.

These social issues in Sylhet and Bengal ultimately contributed to the idea of creating an independent Muslim country.

A well-known Bengali Muslim story recounts the siege of Titumir's fort on November 19, 1831, by British forces led by Major Scott, Lieutenant Shakespeare, and Major Sutherland. The fort's resistance was eventually breached. Titumir and his comrades lost their lives. This story symbolizes the inspiration for an independent Muslim Bengal.

On March 29, 1857, at Barrackpore, Sepoy Mangal Pandey's attack on his British officers marked a significant event in British history. The British Government's response was to temporarily ban the recruitment of soldiers from Bengal, which had a lasting impact on military recruitment in Bengal during World War I.

The Bengal Tenancy Act of 1885 angered Muslim Mirasdar, Malik, and Lords, leading to attacks on British interests. In retaliation, the British Crown seized the property of Muslim Mirasdar and Maliks, which was subsequently auctioned to Hindus for a ninety-nine-year lease with a promissory note of financial aid and military support.

Muslim Lords objected to using the term "Proza" for poor Muslims in East Bengal due to their belief in the Muslim Brotherhood. The British Crown labeled Muslim Mirasdar and

Malik as rebellious terrorists, prompting Muslims to be discouraged from attending the mosque.

In late 1899, Lord Curzon held an unofficial meeting with Muslim nobles, including my great-grandfather, Muhammed Hasim. Lord Curzon acknowledged the social stigma in Sylhet and assured them that the British Crown would listen to their concerns. My great-grandfather emphasized that violence was not the answer, but the partition of Bengal would be acceptable, provided it was peaceful.

Lord Curzon kept his promise, and on October 16, 1905, Bengal was partitioned into two West Bengal and East Bengal. The Hindus mourned this decision, fasting and observing a general strike, while Muslims celebrated the news.

On December 30, 1906, the Muslim League was established, as promised to Lord Curzon.

In 1911, the British Government revoked the partition of Bengal, responding to pressure from wealthy Hindus. The capital was moved from Calcutta to Delhi, reuniting East and West Bengal. This decision led to Muslim activists renewing their quest for an independent Muslim Bengal.

In 1935, the British Crown introduced a democratic election system in an attempt to ease tensions between Muslims and Hindus in Bengal.

In the 1937 election, the Muslim League and Krishak Praja Party formed a coalition government, making Abul Kasem Fazlul Huq the first Prime Minister of Bengal.

On March 23, 1940, Abul Kasem Fazlul Huq indirectly declared the independence of a Muslim country in the Indian subcontinent by presenting a two-nation theory. While Maulana Azad rejected this theory and called for Muslim unity within a united India, history, according to the author, proved that Pakistan was not the solution for Muslims.

On August 16, 1946, the Calcutta Killings occurred as a result of Direct Action Day, orchestrated by Jinnah, leading to violence between Muslims and Hindus in Calcutta. This event made Jinnah realize the difficulties in achieving Pakistan under the upcoming Governor-General.

On August 14, 1947, Jinnah created Pakistan in a closed-door agreement with Mountbatten, possibly driven by his desire to become a Governor-General, a title he deeply admired.

On September 11, 1948, Jinnah passed away, leaving Pakistan in a state of political upheaval, social unrest, economic uncertainty, religious intolerance, and regional tensions. This raises the question of how he became the father of a nation when the nation was burdened with such challenges.

A short note from my desk about India and Pakistan's Independence:

Independence Day of Pakistan on 14 August 1947 and India's Independence Day from Britain on 15 August 1947 is an excruciating, painful memory for millions of people in the Indian Subcontinent. During this, the mobs committed unforgivable sins and atrocities in the name of religion, which witnessed a terrifying memory of loot, rape, murder, and land acquisition. Millions of Hindu Raja and Zaminders' Proza became landowners and millionaires by looting and land acquisition by putting the Muslim reputation under the feet of the world.

I am the grandson of a Muslim League founding member and son of a late Muslim League leader who was "The Peace Committee Standing Committee Chairman" in 1971 East Pakistan. I know exactly what happened in the Indian Subcontinent.

India and Pakistan retained King George VI as head of both states until India transitioned to a Republic following American Republicism when the Constitution of India came into effect on 26 January 1950, celebrated as the Indian Republic, replaced the Dominion of India with the enactment of the sovereign of India.

Most Indian believe India gained independence following the independence movement through non-violent resistance and civil disobedience. However, it was not true. Great Britain had to withdraw because, in WWII, it lost 384,000 soldiers in combat but a higher number of colonial soldiers. Britain calculated it could not sustain 584 princely states, British India and its 17 provinces.

By the end of the War, Britain's debt exceeded 200 percent of GDP. Britain needed to continue to import food with industrial production turned over to wartime needs; there needed to be more export sales to cover the costs. In 1946, Britain took a loan for $586 million and a further $3.7 billion line of credit. To the total loan of $US3.75bn, Canada contributed another US$1.19 bn, both at 2% annual interest.

By the end of World War II, Britain had a huge debt burden of £21 billion. Much of this was held in foreign hands, with around £3.4 billion being owed overseas mainly to creditors in the United States, representing around one-third of annual GDP. In other words, Great Britain was broke. It could not sustain an efficient government in India.

The partition of India, in which British India was divided along religious lines into the Dominions of India and Pakistan, was accompanied by violent riots, mass casualties, and the displacement of nearly 15 million people. Practically, there was no Indian Independence; the bloodiest partition created pain, not joy of victory.

The main reason the Muslim League demanded Pakistan was

to liberate named Proza Muslims from Hindu Raja and Zamindars, not for Islam. In Pakistani and Bangladeshi culture, 99.9% of so-called Muslims do not even know the main principle of Islam, "Monotheism," and that guaranteed vast majority do not practice the second most important pillar in Islam, five times prayer. And Bengalis are proud to be Bengali and dance on dead Muslim bodies. Ironically, the Muslim League was created in Dhaka.

President Ayub Khan

On October 27, 1958, an Army General from West Pakistan declared a military takeover, greeted with warmth by the Pakistan Muslim League, a Sunni stronghold, who expressed relief that Pakistan had been saved. In contrast, the Pakistan Muslim League (Jinnah) and other political parties condemned the military intervention.

The close relationship developed between the Pakistan Muslim League and Ayub Khan was characterized by mutual respect and political guidance sought by Ayub Khan from the traditional Muslim Leaguers.

From 1947 to 1958, Pakistan grappled with a significant political crisis, prompting the necessary military intervention by Ayub Khan. East Pakistan, with strong support for socialism and provincial autonomy, posed challenges for the Islamic Republic of Pakistan. The Muslim Leaguers (Jinnah), primarily Aga Khani, sought to reinstate the Governor-Generalship under the British Crown and promote secularism, while the Pakistan Muslim League aimed for an Islamic Republic with semi-autonomous provinces and complete independence from the British Crown.

Recognizing the need to educate the people about the electoral process, my father advised President Ayub Khan to implement a basic democracy By creating and establishing a Village governmental system. However, President Ayub Khan expressed concerns about the associated costs and instead opted to create over five thousand Union Presidencies in East Pakistan.

During Ayub Khan's Presidency, Pakistan's economy reached its peak, owing to the advice of astute Muslim Leaguers who encouraged a focus on industrialization, education, and agricultural investment. This development drew envy from the British Crown and India, leading British Intelligence Agent Thomas Williams to craft a memorandum with six points and hand it to Mujib.

Following the demise of his primary mentor, Huseyn Shaheed Suhrawardy, on December 5, 1963, Mujib, facing multiple legal cases under the martial law administration, sought legal expertise in London, guided by his close friend Tazuddin Ahmed.

In response to changing political dynamics, Mujib presented the six points to the subject committee on February 5, 1966, advocating for their inclusion in the conference agenda the following day. However, the committee rejected the six points, branding Sheikh Mujibur Rahman as a separatist, a claim he vehemently denied.

Mujib's subsequent arrest on May 8, 1966, under the Defence of Pakistan Act and on alleged charges of the Agartala Conspiracy, was interpreted by the Awami League as an attempt to silence the underrepresented Bengali voice.

Sheikh Mujibur Rahman's release on February 22, 1969, marked by an unsettled court-martial case, was embraced by Dhaka University students who hailed him as "Bongobondhu."

On March 25, 1969, President Ayub Khan's resignation, prompted by humiliation in both East and West Pakistan, signified a stark departure from his once esteemed position as the savior of a United Pakistan, leaving the nation on the brink of dissolution.

Nucleus Movement

The Nucleus Movement, led by Serajul Alam Khan, was a clandestine organization within the East Pakistan Chhatra League faction that played a pivotal role in the dismantling of United Pakistan.

According to authentic information gathered from private conversations between my father and his associates, an intelligence report from East Pakistan's ISI in 1970 suggested that Dr. Gobindra Chandra Dev was the mastermind behind the secretive Nucleus organization. Dev was actively involved in monitoring the movement, promoting the Bengali Cultural Revolution, and maintaining strong connections with the Calcutta Bhadralok. Notably, a small group had been actively fostering Bengali nationalism, particularly by commemorating Hindu religious events in schools and colleges from 1948 to 1969.

Online sources detail Dev's early academic achievements and positions. He commenced his career as a lecturer at Ripon College in Kolkata, later moving to Dinajpur during World War II when the college was relocated. Despite the college's return to Kolkata in 1945, Dev chose to remain in Dinajpur as the founding principal of the newly established branch of Surendranath College (now Dinajpur Government College).

Joining the Department of Philosophy at Dhaka University in July 1953, Dev also served as the house tutor of Dhaka Hall (present Shahidullah Hall) in 1957 before assuming the role of provost at Jagannath Hall the same year. In the late 1960s, he taught as a visiting professor at Wilkes-Barre College in Pennsylvania, USA, and in 1963, he was appointed as the chairman of the Department of Philosophy, eventually becoming a full professor on July 1, 1967.

In honor of Dev's humanist philosophy, his admirers established "The Govinda Dev Foundation" for the World Brotherhood. Moreover, Dev's active involvement in the Pakistan Philosophical Congress, serving as its General Secretary in the 1960s until his demise in 1971, underscored his dedication to intellectual and cultural pursuits. His establishment of a Philosophy House at Dhaka University further solidified his commitment to promoting and practicing his life-oriented and humanist philosophy.

The term "nucleus" typically refers to the cell nucleus in biology, which is the membrane-bound organelle housing the chromosomes and genetic information, controlling the cell's growth and reproduction.

Regarding the controversy surrounding the Nucleus Movement, conflicting information has arisen. While Serajul Alam Khan claimed to have initiated the movement in 1962, his former student activists ASM Abdur Rab and Shahjahan Siraj presented contradictory accounts, including in TV interviews available on YouTube.

Based on my assessment, it is conceivable that Serajul Alam Khan may have established a connection with Dr. Gobindra Chandra Dev, who also served as a house tutor at Dhaka Hall. It is possible that their interaction occurred during a tutoring session.

However, it is unlikely that Serajul Alam Khan single-handedly conceived the Nucleus Movement, as it appears that Dr. Gobindra Chandra Dev played a pivotal role as its mastermind.

In my evaluation, it is apparent that Tofail Ahmed, Serajul Alam Khan, ASM Abdur Rab, and Shahjahan Siraj are all involved in dishonest practices, rendering them unreliable sources. Notably, Serajul Alam Khan has claimed responsibility for initiating the "**Joy Bangla**" slogan in 1969, highlighting the significance of these individuals in the political history of Bangladesh.

Tofail Ahmed titled Sheikh Mujibur Rahman **"Bangabandhu."** Some accused him of declaring Mujib as **Bangabandhu** because of his affair with one of Mujib's daughters to impress his daughters. He was also accused of having an affair with one of Mujib's daughters while Mujib was in jail. Only God knows the truth about why he declared Mujib **"Bangabandhu."**

ASM Abdur Rab raised the **Bangladeshi Flag** at Dhaka

University on March 2, 1971. Shahjahan Siraj declared Bangladesh's independence on March 3, 1971, and Mujib is the **Father of Bengali**. However, Serajul Alam Khan, ASM Abdur Rab and Shahjahan Siraj later formed Jatiya Samajtantrik Dal (JSD), which is in contradiction with Bengali nationalism.

The original organizer of the Nucleus Movement is still being determined except for the intelligence speculation about **Dr. Gobindra Chandra Dev**. He was financially sound and socially established to have elite support.

Serajul Alam Khan is taking credit for his absence because, in 1971, the Pakistan military killed him during the Searchlight Operation.

Mujib

"Dead "Bangabandhu" is more powerful than live **"Bangabandhu." Chief Justice Hasan Foez Siddique 1/1/2022**

Bangladeshi Bengali highly revered Mujib as their iconic leader. Talking about Mujib is highly dangerous in Bangladesh. If you speak about Mujib in Bangladesh, your life would be in great danger. High possibility of being a subject of a targeted killing.

According to the BBC 2004 polls, the BBC announced Sheikh Mujibur Rahman, the Greatest Bengali of all time, voted by Bengalis worldwide.

In late 2011, Journalist Sagar Sarowar and I discussed creating an informative Debunk 71 documentary YouTube movie. On the morning of February 11, 2012, he and his wife were murdered in his Dhaka residency. The Bangladesh Government did not conduct a thorough criminal investigation to find the real motive for his murder. His murder proves that it is impossible to talk or write about the pros and cons of 1971 and Mujib in Bangladesh.

However, I will briefly tell you about Mujib, which I heard from my childhood to college life from Mujib's close people and people whom a few times met with him. In the late 1940s, Mujib used to bring tea to the Huseyn Shaheed Suhrawardy office during the Muslim League Leaders' coffee table conversations or meetings.

During the Hindu-Muslim riot in Calcutta, Mujib looted wealthy Hindu families' wealth. He used to know wealthy Hindu families because his father was a tea boy in a prominent Hindu lawyer's office. After creating Pakistan, he built a big house with looted money in Dhaka.

In 1948, he managed to have a fake college certificate admitted to Dhaka University. Still, Dhaka University identified Mujib's fraudulent certificate. He was expelled from the university. At the request of Huseyn Shaheed Suhrawardy, Dhaka University reversed the decision and made it rusticate instead.

Huseyn Shaheed Suhrawardy needed Mujib for his political interest in the Faridpur district. According to the election ethics committee, an expelled student from the university on the ground of fraud will automatically disqualify Mujib from running for the Assembly Faridpur seat; that's the exact reason Huseyn Shaheed Suhrawardy wanted a political rusticate for Mujib, not expelled on the ground of fraud.

According to the East Pakistan financial banking fraud case, Mujib had twenty fraudulent bank loan documents where he claimed he was the minister of twenty East Pakistani ministries. In 1954, the provincial election Mujib elected in the Provincial Assembly that Government lasted approximately two years. There is no evidence that Mujib was a full minister in the cabinet.

However, Mujib was accused of murdering Deputy Speaker Shahed Ali Patwary during the East Pakistan Assembly Session on 23 September 1958. The murder case was the biggest cover-up in Pakistan's history. Everyone saw Mujib kill him, but no one came out as a witness.

From 1948 to 66, Mujib helped thousands of Bengali people to take Hindu abandoned houses by threatening Hindus to leave East Pakistan; his group earned the nickname **"Mujib Bhahini."**

He also helped Dhaka University students to find lodges or roommates in the city. At the university, he was nicknamed "Mujib Vehi." That's how he won the hearts and minds of the Bengali people in Dhaka. In reality, he was a goon.

What Mujib said and what Bengalis are saying about Mujib is contradictory. Mujib was the All-Pakistan Awami League, not the Bengali leader. In 1955, the Pakistan Muslim League, Krishak Sramik Party, Awami League, and all major East Pakistan political parties declared the "Islamic Republic of Pakistan." There was no political objection to the "Islamic Republic of Pakistan" declaration by Mujib. In 1962, the Awami League supported the Muslim League (Jinnah) in the Union election, and in the 1965 United Pakistan presidential election was when Fatima Jinnah was running for the United Pakistan Presidency. Mujib was the campaign manager in East Pakistan for Fatima Jinnah's campaign.

1970 Election

Regarding the 1971 war, both Bangladeshi Bengali and Pakistan military factions have been accused of propagating misleading narratives, exhibiting characteristics akin to pathological lying. Bangladeshi Bengali efforts in indoctrinating the masses about the 1971 war have drawn comparisons to the tactics observed in North Korea.

A critical element that both Bangladeshis and Pakistanis must acknowledge is that the root cause of the war was the 1970 election, a point widely supported by various political commentators. The 1970 election was a subject of intense controversy among political parties, with certain Pakistani leaders accusing President Yahya Khan of colluding with Mujib to secure the presidency for himself and the prime ministership for Mujib. Additionally, some advocated for an election boycott in response to the national cyclone disaster on November 3, 1970, while others rejected participation in the election under military rule.

In the wake of President Yahya Khan's mishandling of the cyclone disaster, the Muslim League council, Awami League senior leaders, and Awami Bhashani (Socialist) vehemently criticized his actions, with Awami Bhashani interpreting the mishandling as discriminatory against East Pakistani Bengalis.

Despite these circumstances, Mujib welcomed the election and agreed to the general election for the National Assembly and provincial Assemblies. He pledged to participate in the drafting and ratification of a new Pakistan constitution with the consensus of all provinces following a United Pakistan election.

During the negotiations between President Yahya Khan and Mujib, there was no mention of Mujib's desire for a Confederation Union or an independent country. Documented accounts indicate that his six points were merely a political bargaining tool against President Ayub Khan's one-unit presidential system and dictatorial rule, with Mujib consistently advocating for a strong Federal Pakistan Government. He also made a solemn oath by the Quran, vowing not to dismantle Pakistan but rather to fortify it and honor the ratified new constitution upon its parliamentary approval.

A critical observation is that from 1967 to 1970, Dhaka City remained under the control of Mujib Bahini, with Mujib consolidating his influence in Dhaka University. However, it should be noted that Nawab Salimullah originally established the university to provide higher education to Muslims in East Bengal, Assam, and Tripura, but it was later transformed into a mini-cantonment by Mujib during 1948-56 and 1966-1970.

Furthermore, it is noteworthy that while Mujib was not a Dhaka University student, he frequented Madhur Canteen regularly, ostensibly leveraging Dhaka University students for his political aspirations.

Amidst these events, one positive aspect of Mujib's actions was his assistance in finding lodging or roommates for students from remote villages at Dhaka University, thereby cultivating political allies who would later prove instrumental during the 1969 insurrection and the 1970 election. These allies emotionally rallied behind Mujib, perpetuated rumors and falsehoods, stuffed the ballot box, and heralded him as Bangabandhu and the father of the Bengali nation.

Some Bengali individuals have fervently argued that the 1970 election served as a referendum for Bangladesh's Independence. However, the reality remains that in 1970, less than five percent of East Pakistani Bengalis were literate due to the oppressive two-century Hindu Zamindar rule.

While acknowledging the lack of awareness among the new generation stemming from various factors such as familial background and disinformation, I draw upon my intimate knowledge of the 1970 election derived from my father and relatives' involvement as political candidates for the National and Provincial Assembly. It is important to rectify the misconception that Pakistanis sought to subjugate Bengalis systematically, treating them as slaves, an erroneous perspective that has contributed to the vilification of Pakistanis in the eyes of many Bengalis. It is crucial to recognize that East Pakistan, constituting the majority, was located thousands of miles away from West Pakistan and played an instrumental role in the creation of Pakistan in 1946, a vision that had its seeds sown in 1911.

The 1971 War

The 1971 war stands as a source of immense pride for Bangladeshi Bengalis, representing one of the most significant triumphs in their millennia-long history. However, nevertheless, the war's political characterization remains unsealed, with various interpretations ranging from mystery to tragedy, liberation to independence, civil war, West Pakistan's betrayal, or a meticulously executed Indian intelligence operation, depending on one's perspective.

General MAG Osmani, the War General, referred to it as a "mystery," as he had limited knowledge of the 1971 war until he crossed into India in late April.

To my father, it was a testament to the betrayal of the Pakistan military. The Communist Party viewed it as a political-strategic error because they aspired to launch a communist revolution in United Pakistan. For the Bangladeshi Nationalist Party, it represented liberation, especially since their leader, Major Zia, rebelled against the Pakistani military's searchlight operation, aiming to protect East Pakistanis from impending army atrocities.

In the eyes of RAW (India's external intelligence agency), it was a successful intelligence operation labeled A-Z. For many Awami Leaders, it was a tragedy, as they had been preparing for Federalism with provincial autonomy.

Within the Awami League, three distinct groups emerged. The first group, known as the Old Awami, were Federalists advocating for a United Pakistan with provincial autonomy. They were the founding members of the Awami Muslim League, having previously been aligned with the Muslim League. The second group, Awami Bhashani, affiliated with the National Awami Party (NAP), held socialist ideals and aimed for socialism in Pakistan. The third group, Awami Mujib Bahini, comprised Dhaka University Students, Hindu minorities, RAW Agents, and prominent local goons.

It is known that between 1948 and 1966, Mujib was a well-known local figure or "goon" in Dhaka, earning him the moniker "Mujib Vahi." During this period, he was often hired to engage in disputes and invasions related to Hindu abandoned properties, serving as a thug in various conflicts. Huseyn Shaheed Suhrawardy extended his legal and political protection.

Dhaka University students played a pivotal role in transforming Mujib into a political icon in 1969, bestowing upon him the titles of "Mujib Vahi" and eventually "Bangabandhu." Mujib assisted these students in finding accommodation, and roommates, covering admission fees, and obtaining food. Given that many of these students hailed from remote villages, Mujib Vahi became their primary source of support in Dhaka City. It is well-documented that most elected student government leaders from Dhaka University would regularly dine at Mujib's house.

However, Mujib was a goon, not a student political activist; his admission to Dhaka University was marred by fraudulent certificates, leading to a subsequent expulsion. As a matter of fact, under the influence of Huseyn Shaheed Suhrawardy, the decision was reversed, and Mujib received a political rustication, which was necessary to facilitate his participation in the East Pakistan Assembly elections.

Allegedly Agartala Conspiracy was the Bangladesh Independence Movement, and there was a thorough investigation of the Agartala Conspiracy. Pakistan's Government's failure to link Mujib made Dhaka University students angry, which led to massive protests.

The Agartala Conspiracy was one of the few documented instances of his involvement in dismembering Pakistan. While Pakistan's government thoroughly investigated the Agartala Conspiracy, they failed to establish a direct link between Mujib and the conspiracy.

Although Mujib was aware of the conspirators, he never disclosed their identities to the government. Notably, during the Agartala Conspiracy meeting, Mujib did not express a desire for an independent country; it was Tajuddin Ahmad who attempted to convince him of this path.

According to reliable sources, the mastermind behind the creation of Bangladesh was I.B. Agent Serajul Alam Khan, code-named "DADA," who led the East Pakistan war alongside West Pakistan. Four groups actively contributed to the Bangladesh independence movement:

1. RAW agents: After India's 1965 war, Prime Minister Indira Priyadarshini Gandhi was determined to take action. She held a confidential meeting with trusted individuals, including Colonel Nanon, Journalist Banerjee, and the code-named Red Flag (possibly Jyoti Basu). It was in 1968 that the Intelligence Bureau (I.B.) was split into external and internal intelligence agencies due to India's poor performance in the 1962 border war with China.

2. Hindu Minority: The Hindu minority in East Pakistan endured significant hardships from 1946 to 1966, involving looting, rape, and forceful land acquisition by Mujib Bahini. The anger and desire for retribution among Hindu former Raja and Zamindars resulted in their active participation during 1969-1971.

3. Dhaka University students played a critical role in raising the Bengali flag at Dhaka University on March 2, 1971. Their actions, notably led by Chhatra League leaders, contributed to the proliferation of the "Joy Bangla" and

"Joy Bangabandhu" slogans, ultimately advancing the Bangladesh independence movement.

4. Goons of Dhaka in East Pakistan took advantage of the political turmoil from 1969 to 1971, engaging in looting rampage, rape, murder, and land seizures under the banner of Mujib.

In 1969, President Ayub Khan was urged to transfer power to a civilian patriot, a recommendation he declined, leading to his handover of power to General Yahya Khan. This choice would later be viewed as a significant blunder. It is well-documented that General Yahya Khan was frequently intoxicated.

General Yahya Khan formed a political coalition that included Mujib, Bhutto, Jamaat-e-Islami, and Nejami Islami, excluding socialists and the Muslim League. In contrast, President Ayub Khan had close ties to Muslim League leaders dating back to 1958.

The abovementioned political chronological event and situation contributed to the chaos in East Pakistan and broke out the war like scenario.

Chapter Four
Countdown to the 71 War

On February 22, 1969, Sheikh Mujibur Rahman, the leader of the All-Pakistan Awami League, was released from what can only be described as a bizarre imprisonment within the Dhaka army cantonment. His arrival at his Dhanmondi residence was met with an emotional reunion with his families and supporters, with thousands of his followers accompanying him during the procession, making him an iconic leader.

At this release followed a peculiar court-martial trial procedure, an unprecedented event in the history of the country. A civilian was expected to undergo a trial in a criminal court procedure, not a court-martial.

Earlier, on May 8, 1966, Mujib had been arrested under the Defence of Pakistan Act on unfounded charges related to the Agartala Conspiracy. The conspiracy alleged that Mujib, along with thirty-four other conspirators from the armed forces and civil administration, had planned to orchestrate an armed secession of East Pakistan from the rest of United Pakistan with the support of the Indian military. It was argued by the Government of Field Marshal Mohammad Ayub Khan that Mujib had earlier traveled to Agartala in India to solicit Indian support for his scheme of breaking up United Pakistan.

As a matter of fact, although Mujib was present at the meeting, he had rejected the conspiracy, advocating instead for the mobilization of the autonomous movement.

The Agartala Conspiracy was initially leaked by the Daily Nishan, a small newspaper based in Malibag, Dhaka, in early December 1965. While the newspaper could not provide a detailed account of the Agartala meeting's exact nature, it hinted at the emergence of "A New Country." Pakistan's Intelligence (ISI) attempted to verify the report's authenticity, but the editor declined to disclose the source of the information, suggesting involvement from the Awami Mujib group.

The Pakistani government initially maintained silence regarding the Agartala meeting. However, President Ayub broke the silence in 1966, following Mujib's announcement of his Six-Point plan, which advocated for confederation autonomy within a federal Pakistan. Ayub's stern declaration that supporters of the six-point movement would be treated as enemies of Pakistan under the Defence of Pakistan Act garnered significant attention in the newspapers across East Pakistan, effectively providing Mujib and his movement with invaluable publicity.

The unresolved Agartala conspiracy case swiftly propelled Mujib to fame in East Pakistan, further bolstering the visibility of his Six Points. Rumors and hearsay about Mujib and his six points spread rapidly among the illiterate villagers and college students, contributing to the momentum of Mujib's burgeoning movement.

All Parties Roundtable Meetings

In 1969, President Ayub Khan organized the "Round Table Conference," inviting all political parties from East Pakistan and West Pakistan to deliberate on a sustainable political solution for a United Pakistan. During the conference, Jamaat-e-Islami leader Abul A'la Maududi proposed the establishment of a ninety-day caretaker governmental system to ensure a free and fair election.

However, the proposal faced opposition from the United Pakistan Muslim League, which was against the idea of a caretaker government. They instead advocated for handing over power to an East Pakistan General, citing concerns about potential Indian aggression and the need to appease the East Pakistani movement. The All-Pakistan Awami League pressed for the transfer of power to a civilian patriot, aligning with the wishes of the military leadership in Pakistan. Meanwhile, the Pakistan People's Party, led by Zulfikar Ali Bhutto, declined to attend the roundtable conference and demanded the immediate resignation of President Ayub Khan. Bhutto also called for robust anti-Ayub demonstrations across the country.

In 1969, East Pakistan witnessed a surge of violence, riots, looting, murders, and gang rapes orchestrated by Dhaka University Students, Awami Bhasani, and Mujib's Bahini, the local goons. The deteriorating law and order situation prompted the East Pakistan

Police force to declare a state of collapse. During a public meeting, Mujib asserted that he was the de facto ruler of East Pakistan.

The origin of East Pakistan violence began on January 4, 1969, when left-wing students were organized. The joining groups were the East Pakistan Student Union (Matia), East Pakistan Chhatra League, East Pakistan Student Union (Menon), and the Dhaka University Student Union. Primarily, they demanded Eleven Points.

They called for a strike on January 20, 1969, throughout East Pakistan. Amanullah Asaduzzaman, a student, was killed by East Pakistan Police, which led to more strikes, demonstrations and violence from 21 to January 24.

On January 24, 1969, the violence intensified; two more protesters were killed in Mymensingh. Many were injured throughout the East Pakistan. East Pakistan was shaken by violence. Approximately 61 people were killed during the intense violence that was the beginning of a vicious culture of violence that lasted until 1975.

Simultaneously, in West Pakistan, the Pakistan People's Party (PPP) led formidable anti-Ayub Khan protests, street demonstrations, and riots against Ayub Khan's government. The increase in prices of essential food items such as sugar, tea, and wheat further fueled public discontent, with people vocally expressing their disapproval by chanting "Down with Ayub Khan" and employing derogatory terms to refer to Ayub.

The streets of major cities in West Pakistan were marked with widespread wall chalking featuring pejorative and defamatory remarks aimed at Ayub, garnering significant attention in the West Pakistan news media. In response to the growing unrest, Home and Defence Minister Vice-Admiral Rahman informed journalists that the country was succumbing to mob rule, with the police forces struggling to effectively manage the situation.

President Ayub Khan Resign

On March 25, 1969, President Ayub Khan resigned from the presidency and transferred power to General Yahya Khan, the Commander-in-Chief, with the aim of restoring stability. General Yahya Khan promptly enforced martial law and pledged to conduct a free and fair election once law and order were reestablished in both East Pakistan and West Pakistan.

General Yahya Khan's Presidency & War 71

On March 25, 1969, General Yahya Khan was inaugurated as the President of United Pakistan. He inherited a two-decade-long constitutional crisis in the country. He imposed martial law administration, declaring martial law nationwide, with the promise of conducting a free and fair election, ratifying a new constitution, and transferring power to a newly elected civilian head of state, whether President or Prime Minister.

The regional and national political situation was not in his favor. Inter-provincial racial tension existed between the Punjabi-Pashtun-Mohajir-dominated West Pakistan and the ethnically Bengali-Bihari (Mohajir) and Punjabi population in East Pakistan.

It must be noted that Jinnah created a national ideological crisis in 1947 by declaring secularism, whereas Pakistan was created based on Muslim Nationalism. He was advised to form the Islamic Republic of Pakistan instead of centralization based on secularism. He arrogantly disrespected the advice of senior Muslim Leaguers, declared a secular state of Pakistan, and made the British Crown Head of Pakistan, which was a significant blow to Pakistan's unity. Because of Jinnah, the Muslim League lost popularity and has never fully regained it to this day.

Some Muslim Leaguers broke away from the Muslim League due to Jinnah's arrogance. In June 1949, the Awami Muslim

League was formed under Abdul Hamid Khan Bhashan. Bhashani, in his speech during the formation of the Awami Muslim League, said, "Awami Muslim League is a Sallam (Goodbye) to Jinnahism, not Muslimism." The Muslim League council, led by Khwaja Nazimuddin, struggled to reunite the Muslim League, but many cursed Jinnah for the chaos in the Muslim League.

Secondly, Jinnah gave a speech declaring that "Urdu would be Pakistan's official language." He publicly stated, "Whoever opposes the idea of the official language Urdu is an enemy of Pakistan." He did not allow anyone to democratically debate the language issue, which was a dictatorial approach. Jinnah created problems and passed them on to President Yahya Khan.

President Yahya Khan attempted to resolve Pakistan's constitutional crisis by returning to the pre-1958 political structure. While the political decision was correct, it came too late and was irreversible. A systematic approach was needed to dcfuse political violence, such as drafting a new constitution and holding a referendum on it. This would have served two purposes: first, diverting public attention from street demonstrations and protests towards open political discourse, and second, returning to normal economic activities.

President Yahya Khan abolished the parity principle in the hope that a larger share for East Pakistan in the Assembly would satisfy the East Pakistani ethnic and regional majority and ensure Pakistan's unity. However, the dissolution of the centralized government did not lead to a positive outcome for both East Pakistan and West Pakistan, as anticipated. Instead of appeasing the Bengalis, it intensified violence, looting, targeted killings, and gang rapes.

Cyclone Bhola 1970

The 1970 Bhola cyclone was a devastating tropical cyclone that struck East Pakistan and India's West Bengal on November 11, 1970. It was one of the deadliest tropical cyclones ever recorded and one of the world's deadliest natural disasters. While most political parties demanded the suspension of the November general election to aid the cyclone victims, Mujib instead requested the postponement of the election.

According to various sources and authentic information, the Chittagong DC informed President Yahya Khan that the situation was under control. There were reports of some minor incidents, but upon hearing this, President Yahya Khan canceled his trip to Chittagong and accepted Mujib's demand to postpone the election. In reality, the DC was held at gunpoint by Awami goons to prevent President Yahya Khan's visit to Chittagong, allowing the Awami League to capitalize on the Cyclone's disaster for their political advantage.

The Awami League's politicization of the cyclone was one of the heinous crimes committed by the party. It was an unforgivable sin, and there should be a criminal investigation of the 1970 cyclone incident in East Pakistan. The disinformation spread during that time caused a volcanic hatred between East Pakistan and West Pakistan.

1970 General Elections

On July 28, 1969, President Yahya Khan formulated a framework for the general elections in United Pakistan to be held in November 1970. However, due to a cyclone disaster in East Pakistan, the election was postponed to December 7, 1970, at the demand of Awami Mujib, to elect members of the National Assembly.

The highly controversial election was held on December 7, 1970, marking the first general election in Pakistan's history and the only one held as United Pakistan. Voting took place in 300 constituencies, with 162 in East Pakistan and 138 in West Pakistan.

My father was a candidate for the National Assembly from the Muslim League Council. Until his death, he always maintained that the election was rigged. In our village voting center, not even ten people cast their votes. However, the Awami League candidate received a high number of votes in my father's constituency. My father claimed that high school and college kids sealed the ballots instead of the rightful voters.

We must understand that our people were largely illiterate, and women were only allowed to go outside the houses with valid reasons. Women going out was considered a shameful act, so the idea of them casting votes was beyond imagination. However, my father sent a few trusted women to investigate fourteen villages to determine whether women were voting that day. It was found that hardly any respected Muslim family women had voted, except for a few poor women. One woman even confessed to my father that she had sealed one hundred ballot books for a few hundred Taka.

The general election took place all over United Pakistan. In East Pakistan, the Eight Parties coalition led by the Awami Mujib secured almost all seats, while they won no seats in West Pakistan's four provinces. The socialist Pakistan People's Party (PPP) won the exclusive mandate in the four provinces of West Pakistan but failed to secure any seats in East Pakistan. The Pakistan Democratic League (PDL), led by Nurul Amin, won a single seat in East Pakistan but none in West Pakistan, representing the only non-Awami party in East Pakistan. However, it failed to gain the mandate to create a coalition government.

The Awami League won 160 seats, giving them the absolute political right to form a government for five years, having secured victory in East Pakistan. The socialist PPP gained 81 seats, allowing them to serve as an opposition party for five years. The conservative Pakistan Muslim League (PML) secured ten seats in the National Assembly, disqualifying them from becoming the opposition.

The general election resulted in a severe political crisis for United Pakistan rather than a solution. The fear and anxiety increase among Muslim Leaguers. Muslim Leaguers were obnoxious about

Mujib for many reasons. As far as I heard from some Muslim League leaders, these concerns were:

- No. 1, Mujib Agartala conspiracy case unsettled.
- No.2, Mujib 6 points. Mujib never publicly acknowledged who authored it. Regarding Six Points, Mujib always remained silent.
- No.3, Mujib had 20 financial Bank fraud exceptional cases. On the loan application, he wrote that he is the provincial minister for 20 ministries in East Pakistan. He was elected only once for a few months.
- No. 4, inexperience in administrative duties.
- No.5, He was a goon in Dhaka known as Mujib Bahini. Some criminal and murder cases were pending.
- No.6, Indian interference in East Pakistan politics, etc.
- The general election was a dead-end for United Pakistan.

Several trilateral political negotiations were held between Zulfikar Ali Bhutto, President Yahya Khan, and Mujibur Rahman to form a coalition government, aiming to display unity to Pakistan's counterpart, India. However, the delay in the transfer of power led to increased violence and bloodshed on the streets of Dhaka.

President Yahya Khan indirectly inquired about Mujib's intentions through a confidential source, seeking to understand whether Mujib desired an independent country, a concern shared by many generals and Muslim Leaguers. Mujib's response was a resounding "No." He directly conveyed to the informant that the situation was not under his control due to overwhelming pressure from the students.

Mujib emphasized that the only way to manage the crowd was by convening the parliament. However, President Yahya was apprehensive about handing over power to Mujib due to underlying reasons.

Delhi had already recognized Bangladesh, making a U-turn improbable. On March 1, 1971, the National Assembly was scheduled to convene in the parliament. Instead, President Yahya Khan declared martial law indefinitely, effectively extinguishing any hope for a United Pakistan.

I heard that when most of the political parties boycotted the 1970 election, including Mazlum Jono Neta Bhashani, President Yahya Khan got into an awkward situation. To show the world that he was a man of the word, he committed to conduct the election.

He told people that whoever will vote will get 1 KG of Aata (flour) extra in their ration. During the East Pakistan period, all the poor East Pakistanis used to get ration and they used to pay half fare on local trains, known as third-class compartments.

He rented the entire Hotel Continental for the foreign

journalist to show off the "Free and Fair" election.

President Yahya Khan's sweet boys were Mujib and Bhutto. United Pakistani military was taking foreign journalists into the polling booth to show election was "Free and Fair." In front of certain voting centers, all the poor people were lined up for Aata (flour), and journalists took pictures of them.

The foreign journalists said the election was one of the fairest elections in Pakistan's history. President Yahya Khan proudly gave the speech to the nation with pride. Everything changed when he heard that Mujib was directly and indirectly involved with the Agartala Conspiracy.

March 7th Speech

The March 7, 1971, speech of Sheikh Mujibur Rahman at the Ramna Race Course Field in Dhaka remains highly controversial among Bangladeshi Bengali Nationalists, the Bangladeshi Nationalist Party (BNP), and the Bangladesh Communist Party. While Bangladeshi Bengali nationalists claim the speech was a declaration of Independence, both the BNP and the Communist Party reject this assertion.

The background of the March 7th speech is intriguing, as highlighted by Bangladesh founder Serajul Alam Khan's comment, "Mujib is a Doll." He originally authored the 7th March speech. However, Mujib changed some words from the speech.

Upon learning that Mujib was going to give a speech, President Yahya Khan and several Muslim Leaguers dispatched informants to ascertain whether Mujib intended to declare Independence. Mujib assured Dhaka Muslim League Leader Kazi Qader and M A Yousuf that he would not declare Independence.

He emphasized that he had also contributed to the Pakistan movement, stressing that the transfer of power was crucial to thwart the Independence movement. He acknowledged that he could not control the crowd, with the students pressuring him to declare the Independence of Bangladesh. He made it clear that neither the Muslim League nor the generals desired him as the President or

Prime Minister of Pakistan.

Before the night of March 7, students and Tajuddin exerted immense pressure on Mujib to declare Independence. Despite this pressure, Mujib stood firm in his decision not to declare Independence and prepared for his imminent arrest. Following the March 7th speech, Mujib engaged in continuous negotiations with President Yahya Khan until his eventual arrest on March 25. As anticipated, when the military came, Mujib was waiting on his sofa to be arrested.

March 9th, 1971

The nickname "Red Moulana" was attributed to Maulana Bhashani due to his revolutionary Chinese socialist views and stances. During a speech on a stage teeming with thousands of people, Awami Bhashani's party leader put the blame on the Muslim League for various issues. He lent his support to the ongoing non-cooperation and non-violent mass protests in East Pakistan until Yaha Khan addressed the needs of the cyclone victims. Notably, there was no mention of Independence in his speech. I have personally heard his speech on the AP archive.

Searchlight Operation March 25

Operation Searchlight was conducted in the middle of the night on March 25, 1971, known as **Kaal Ratri** (blackout night). It was one of the worst preplanned, miscalculated military genocides against the Hindu minority and rebellious students in East Pakistan. On that night, my father happened to be at the Dhaka Continental Hotel, meeting with Muslim League leaders.

Earlier in March, he had traveled from Sylhet to Dhaka to discuss political developments with the Muslim League leaders. Since Dhaka was approximately one hundred and fifty miles from Sylhet, he had decided to stay in the hotel for a couple of weeks.

If I recall correctly, I overheard from my father's

conversation with his friends that he had gone to sleep after the Isha prayer in his hotel room. Late at night, he heard some gunfire, which led him to wake up, drink a glass of water, and perform wudu before offering two Rakat of prayer. Meanwhile, someone knocked on the door. On asking, "Who is disturbing me in the middle of the night?" he received the response, "I am a Muslim Leaguer from the Chittagong district, Lal Saab, please open the door" (some people used to call my father Lal Saab, Vehi).

Upon opening the door, he found a dozen Pakistani soldiers standing in front of his room. He exclaimed, "How dare you, Mr. Yahya, arrest me in the middle of the night when I am trying to sleep!" A military officer extended his hand to shake my father's hand, a common Muslim cultural gesture. "Moulvi Saab, I am a colonel," he said. "We are not here to arrest you but to request that you leave Dhaka immediately. Intelligence suggests that Indian militaries are hiding in Dhaka University rooms to train students in guerrilla warfare. President Yahya is concerned about your safety and security, which is why we are here to escort you to the train station. A military Jeep will take you to Kamalapur Train Station. You can catch the early morning train to Sylhet."

My father agreed, saying, "That's fine; let me get ready." The military Jeep, with my father and a few other Muslim Leaguers, dropped him off at the Kamalapur train station.

My father mentioned that Dhaka was relatively quieter than on other nights. The train was considerably empty compared to usual days. He regretted having a cabin with his colleagues, remarking, "Tikka Khan made the third-class a first-class; why are we wasting money here." Chittagong Muslim League Leader Muslauddin responded, "We are not paying for this train fare; the military paid for us." To which my father replied, "Muslauddin Saab, this time, the military is paying for us, which is not a good sign. The Indian army can attack us at any moment. The Pakistani military needs funds to fight the enemy." Muslauddin nodded in agreement.

In 1971, my father traveled from Dhaka to Sylhet by train. However, the military mistakenly put my dad on a Chittagong-bound train. He had to change trains at Akhaura Junction to board the local train to Sylhet. He disembarked at Maijgaon Train Station, close to my maternal grandparents' village, KM Tilla. Instead of going to his town, he headed to my grandparents' house. Before his departure to Dhaka, he had left my mother with her family in Maijgaon. After a couple of weeks, he returned home with my mom by boat.

According to my father's account, life around Akhaura Junction seemed normal. People were going about their daily activities. However, there was a notable military presence around the area due to its proximity to the Indian border.

In Maijgaon, people were discussing various things. Some spoke of a major revolt and killings of many military personnel, while others claimed the Indian Army had already entered Dhaka. The rumors in the villages were baseless and illogical, lacking substantial evidence to support the authenticity of the events surrounding the March 25th operation. With no access to radios, televisions, or newspapers and only a few people literate, the spread of baseless rumors was inevitable.

My research revealed that, according to pro-Pakistani elements, the widespread violence resulting from the anti-Ayub movement led to Operation Searchlight and the Bangladesh Liberation War. Bangladesh's architect, Serajul Alam Khan, had allegedly begun moving toward Bangladesh's independence before Mujib's Six-Point movement.

Operation Searchlight undeniably angered the Muslim Leaguers. They felt a strong sense of anger toward the military. Even MAG Osmani, the War General, was a staunch Pakistani and Muslim nationalist. He took up the role of War General for the '71 war due to the atrocities committed during the massacre.

Chapter Five

The Serajul Alam Khan's War

Sizable evidence suggests that the East Pakistan (Bangladesh) independence movement was initially organized in Agartala by Tazuddin Ahmed, known as the Agartala conspiracy. Secondly, it was organized at Dhaka University under the leadership of Serajul Alam Khan on June 6, 1970.

According to authentic documentary evidence, the Searchlight master plan was created in March 1971 by Major General Khadim Hussain Raja, GOC 14th Division, with Major General Rao Farman Ali following up on the decisions made at a meeting of the Pakistan Army staff on February 22. As a result of this meeting, the 16th infantry division from Quetta and the 9th division from Kharian, West Pakistan, were ordered to move to East Pakistan in mid-February.

Some senior Pakistani military officers were unwilling to support the Searchlight Operation, which targeted civilians irrespective of their religious affiliations. Lt. General Shahabzada Yakub Khan, GOC East Pakistan, and East Pakistan's governor, Vice Admiral Syed Mohammad Ahsan, were relieved of their duties for refusing to execute the operation. Lt. Gen. Tikka Khan assumed the governorship and GOC position in East Pakistan.

On March 17, General Raja received the order to execute the Operation over the phone from General Abdul Hamid Khan, Chief of Staff of the Pakistan Army. On March 18, General Raja and Major General Rao Farman Ali discussed the Operation at the GOC's office at Dhaka Cantonment. The entire operation plan spanned 16 paragraphs over five pages.

General Farman briefed the operational principles and conditions for a successful outcome. Simultaneously, General Khadim Raja prepared for the deployment of military units and assigned operational tasks to individual brigades. The military high command speculated that Bengali soldiers might revolt, leading to the order that all Bengali soldiers be disarmed before executing the Operation.

The order to disarm all Bengali soldiers was disturbing, indicating that the high command did not trust the loyalty of East Pakistani soldiers to the Pakistani state. This directive seemed to suggest that East Pakistanis were not considered fully Pakistani and were not expected to defend their own country. However, during the 1965 conflict, the East Bengal Regiment from East Pakistan valiantly fought against India.

Despite this, the high command ordered the arrest of all political leadership without the authorization to use lethal force unless justified. President Yahya Khan was bypassed, and no operational briefing was provided to him.

On March 20, 1971, General Abdul Hamid Khan and Lt. General Tikka Khan reviewed the Searchlight operation plan at the Flagstaff House. Breaking the chain of command under military rules is a serious offense. In this case, General Abdul Hamid Khan assumed the de facto presidency.

Following a comprehensive review of the plan, General Abdul Hamid Khan revised it, ordering the immediate disarmament of the East Pakistan Rifles (EPR), armed police, and other paramilitary forces but not the regular Bengali Army. President Yahya Khan also instructed not to arrest Awami League leaders during a meeting with him, leading to further amendments to the original plan. Subsequently, the high command instructed all military commanders to execute the amended plan.

The Searchlight Operation commenced at 0100 military time on March 26, 1971, in Dhaka. It was conducted as a military surgical operation aimed at minimizing innocent civilian casualties and maximizing the losses of the opposition. The primary target was Dhaka University, with secondary targets being the Hindu minority and Awami League members.

This was a military surgical operation, indicating that all military commanders had sufficient intelligence about their targets. It was not akin to random killings of innocent Bengalis by the

Pakistani military, as believed by some Bangladeshi Bengalis. Those with military training understand that it was a planned military operation and not akin to the targeted killings conducted by rogue elements. However, human errors can occur in all endeavors.

Cabinet Meeting in India

On March 26, 1971, the spymaster and head of the RAW, R.N. Kao, along with Field Marshal Sam Manekshaw MC, Defense Minister Jagjivan Ram, and Prime Minister Indira Priyadarshini Gandhi, held a closed-door meeting officially known as a "Cabinet Meeting" to discuss the potential invasion of East Pakistan on the pretext of genocide.

The decision to invade East Pakistan was unanimous, with the exception of Field Marshal Sam Manekshaw MC, who objected to the idea of launching the invasion during the monsoon season, particularly on March 27, 1971. He put forth a logical argument, citing the difficulties posed by the monsoon season in East Pakistan and the challenges it would present for any military operation. Instead, he proposed training guerrillas to weaken Pakistan, with a plan for the Indian Army to enter Dhaka in November or December.

Declaration of Independence

According to reliable information, the official declaration of independence was made by a junior Pakistan army officer in Chittagong, later identified as Major Zia by the Pakistan military. On March 27, 1971, Major Zia announced Bangladesh's independence on the radio, as can be heard on YouTube. However, there is a general belief among Bengalis that Mujib declared the independence of Bangladesh on March 7th, 1971.

In Jackson Heights, NY, a Bengali individual informed me that his relative acquired the Declaration of Independence from Mujib on March 25 and handed it to Zia. From a logical standpoint, this scenario seems unlikely. Before his arrest, Mujib was surrounded by students and Awami leaders.

The distance from Dhaka to Chittagong is approximately 152 miles, and the roads were less well-developed in 1971 than they are today. The Searchlight Operation was a highly confidential military surgical operation, and even President Yahya was unaware of it. The military initiated the Operation at 0100 military time, indicating shoot-on-sight orders. Major Zia was a sincere, courageous, and professional junior Army officer stationed in Chittagong at the time. It raises questions about how Mujib would have known about him and trusted him to declare the independence of Bangladesh. These stories seem to be fictitious and the **lies** and fabricated, and it is important for history to remain authentic.

While there is widespread misinformation and fabricated narratives about the declaration of Bangladesh's independence and the alleged oppression of Bengalis by the Pakistanis, Major Zia deserves rightful credit for his decisive action in officially declaring independence. In his declaration, he stated, "I, Major Ziaur Rahman, Provincial Head of the government, do hereby declare the Independence of the People's Republic of Bangladesh." Consequently, he became the first President of Bangladesh in political science.

Bangladesh Government

On April 17, 1971, in a village adjacent to the India-Bangladesh border, Baidyanathtala, in the Kushtia district (now Meherpur district), the first Bangladesh Government on East Pakistan soil was formed by the main Agartala Conspirator, Tajuddin Ahmad. Before establishing the government, Tajuddin Ahmed sought confirmation from Golok Bihari Majumder, the D.G. of the Border Security Force (BSF).

In 1971, Golok Bihari Majumder played a crucial role as a fundamental military backup for the Mujibnagar Government against the Pakistani military from day one. Majumder, the then D.G. BSF (Eastern Command), also served as the primary liaison for communicating with the Indian Prime Minister and Defense Minister for the interim government of Bangladesh. During the 1971 war, Majumder served as the primary coordinator of information management on the ground level for guerrilla fighters. Without Golok Bihari Majumder, Bangladesh's liberation war would have been impossible.

Professor Yusuf Ali read the proclamation of Bangladesh Independence, which was drafted by Amir-ul Islam and reviewed by Subrata Roy Chowdhury, a lawyer at the Calcutta High Court. On April 17, 1971, during the ceremony, when asked by a journalist about the name, Tajuddin named the location "Mujibnagar" after

Sheikh Mujibur Rahman. Later, the government-in-exile came to be popularly known as the Mujibnagar Government. Due to fears of a raid by the Pakistani military, Mujibnagar was quickly abandoned after the ceremony's oath. The Government headquarters was then temporarily relocated to Kolkata, first at a house on Ballygunge Circular Road and later at 8 Theatre Road for the rest of the war.

The War

Dhaka University students initiated the 1971 war in the middle of 1970 by escalating violence, looting, and targeted killings in Dhaka. The mobs in Dhaka exploited the ensuing chaos. The lawlessness created confusion among military intelligence and pro-Pakistani elements. In a politically unstable country of 23 years, making a sound political assessment became challenging, resulting in miscalculated political decisions by the Generals.

Major Zia officially declared war in Chittagong on March 27, 1971. This declaration, in text, signified the "Declaration of Independence of Bangladesh." Originally, Serajul Alam Khan had declared the Independence of Bangladesh while addressing a few students in the middle of 1970 and instructed them to create a Bangladeshi flag.

Serajul Alam Khan was known as a mysterious figure. His actions during 1968-71 were unpredictable. He frequently altered his movements to evade arrest by the Pakistani military and had strong connections with India.

Letter from the Acting President of the People's Republic of Bangladesh Syed Nazrul Islam to the President of India, seeking Indian recognition of Bangladesh.

Mujib Nagar, April 24, 1971

Excellency,

Upon the proclamation of the sovereign, independent People's Republic of

Bangladesh, on March 26, 1971, a Government with Sheikh Mujibur Rahman as its head has been established.

A copy of the Proclamation of Independence, Laws Continuance Enforcement Order, and a list of Cabinet Members are enclosed and marked with letters 'A'[1], 'B' and 'C' respectively for the favor of your perusal.

The Government of Bangladesh is exercising full sovereignty and lawful authority within the territories known as East Pakistan prior to March 26, 1971, and has taken all appropriate measures to conduct the business of the State in accordance with custom, usage, and recognized principles of International law.

In view of the friendly relations that traditionally exist between the fraternal peoples of Bangladesh and that of India, I request Your Excellency's Government to accord immediate recognition to the People's Republic of Bangladesh. The Government of Bangladesh will be pleased to establish normal diplomatic relations and exchange envoys with a view to further strengthening the ties of friendship between our two countries.

Please accept, Excellency, the assurances of our highest consideration

(Sd.)

Syed Nazrul Islam

Acting President

(Seal of the Bangladesh Government)

(Sd.)

Khandakar Moshtaque Ahmed,

Foreign Minister

[1] Only 'A' (Proclamation of Independence) is reproduced here as an enclosure to this letter.

Letter from the Acting President of the People's Republic of Bangladesh Syed Nazrul Islam to the President of India, seeking Indian recognition of Bangladesh.

Mujib Nagar, April 24, 1971

Excellency,

Upon the proclamation of the sovereign, independent People's Republic of

Bangladesh, on March 26, 1971, a Government with Sheikh Mujibur Rahman as its head has been established.

A copy of the Proclamation of Independence, Laws Continuance Enforcement Order, and a list of Cabinet Members are enclosed and marked with letters 'A'[1], 'B' and 'C' respectively for the favor of your perusal.

The Government of Bangladesh is exercising full sovereignty and lawful authority within the territories known as East Pakistan prior to March 26, 1971, and has taken all appropriate measures to conduct the business of the State in accordance with custom, usage, and recognized principles of International law.

In view of the friendly relations that traditionally exist between the fraternal peoples of Bangladesh and that of India, I request Your Excellency's Government to accord immediate recognition to the People's Republic of Bangladesh. The Government of Bangladesh will be pleased to establish normal diplomatic relations and exchange envoys with a view to further strengthening the ties of friendship between our two countries.

Please accept, Excellency, the assurances of our highest consideration

Shahinul Islam Khalisdar, EA, MST

(Sd.)

Syed Nazrul Islam

Acting President

(Seal of the Bangladesh Government)

(Sd.)

Khandakar Moshtaque Ahmed,

Foreign Minister

[1] Only 'A' (Proclamation of Independence) is reproduced here as an enclosure to this letter.

Enclosure-A

THE PROCLAMATION OF INDEPENDENCE

Mujib Nagar, Bangladesh

Dated 10th day of April 1971

WHEREAS free elections were held in Bangladesh from 7th December 1970 to 17th January 1971 to elect representatives for the purpose of framing a Constitution,

and

WHEREAS at these elections, the people of Bangladesh elected 167 out of 169 representatives belonging to the Awami League, and

WHEREAS General Yahya Khan summoned the elected representatives of the people to meet on the 3rd March 1971 for the purpose of framing a Constitution,

and

WHEREAS the Assembly so summoned was arbitrarily and illegally postponed for an indefinite period,

and

WHEREAS instead of fulfilling their promise and while still conferring with the representatives of the people of Bangladesh, Pakistan authorities declared an unjust and treacherous war,

and

WHEREAS in the facts and circumstances of such treacherous conduct

Bangabandhu Sheikh Mujibur Rahman, the undisputed leader of 75 million people of Bangladesh, in due fulfillment of the legitimate right of self-determination of the people of Bangladesh, duly made a declaration of independence at Dacca on March 26, 1971, and urged the people of Bangladesh to defend the honor and integrity of Bangladesh,

and

WHEREAS in the conduct of ruthless and savage war, the Pakistani authorities committed and are still continuously committing numerous acts of genocide and unprecedented tortures, amongst others, on the civilian and unarmed people of Bangladesh,

and

WHEREAS the Pakistan Government, by levying an unjust war and committing genocide, and by other repressive measures, made it impossible for the elected representatives of the people of Bangladesh to meet and frame a Constitution and give themselves a Government,

and

WHEREAS the people of Bangladesh, by their heroism, bravery, and revolutionary fervor, have established effective control over the territories of Bangladesh.

We, the elected representatives of the people of Bangladesh, as honor-bound by the mandate given to us by the people of Bangladesh, whose Will is supreme, duly constituted ourselves into a Constituent Assembly, and

having held mutual consultations, and

in order to ensure for the people of Bangladesh equality, human dignity, and social justice,

declare and constitute Bangladesh to be sovereign People's

Republic and thereby confirm the declaration of independence already made by Bangabandhu Sheikh Mujibur Rahman, and

do hereby affirm and resolve that till such time as a Constitution is framed, Bangabandhu Sheikh Mujibur Rahman shall be the President of the Republic and that Syed Nazrul Islam shall be the Vice-President of the Republic, and

that the President shall be the Supreme Commander of all the Armed Forces of the Republic,

shall exercise all the Executive and Legislative powers of the Republic, including the power to grant pardon,

shall have the power to appoint a Prime Minister and such other Ministers as he considers necessary,

shall have the power to levy taxes and expend monies,

shall have the power to summon and adjourn the Constituent Assembly, and **do** all other things that may be necessary to give to the people of Bangladesh an orderly and just Government.

We, the elected representatives of the people of Bangladesh, do further resolve that in the event of there being no President or the President being unable to enter upon his office or being unable to exercise his powers and duties due to any reason whatsoever, the Vice-President shall have and exercise all the powers, duties and responsibilities herein conferred on the President.

We further resolve that we undertake to observe and give effect to all duties

and obligations devolved upon us as a member of the family of nations and by the

Charter of United Nations.

We further resolve that this proclamation of independence shall be deemed to have come into effect from the 26th day of March 1971.

We further resolve that in order to give effect to this instrument, we appoint Prof. M. Yusuf Ali, our duly constituted plenipotentiary, and to give to the President and the Vice-President oaths of office.

(Sd.)

M. Yusuf Ali

Duly Constituted Plenipotentiary

By and under the authority of the

Constituent Assembly of Bangladesh

Dhaka University Muslim Foe

In Bengal, Muslims, intellectuals, political activists, and literateurs emerged as formidable adversaries to the Tagore family and the East Bengal Hindu Zamindar families. Those subscribing to the ideology of Pakistan regarded Rabindranath as a significant obstacle to the establishment of an Islamic culture in East Pakistan. Their primary contention was that Rabindranath's literature and songs were deeply rooted in Hindu polytheistic beliefs, rendering them anti-Islamic.

During the period when Bangladesh constituted East Pakistan, official endeavors were made to expunge Rabindranath from radio, television, and textbooks. This, however, resulted in a significant backlash, leading to the inception of an underground Bengali Nationalist Movement known as the Nucleus Movement. Approximately 38% of the population in East Pakistan identified as Hindus, many of whom were highly educated school and college teachers. They imparted to their students the song "Amar Sonar Bangla," in addition to Pakistan's national anthem.

Efforts by Pro-Pakistani factions to eliminate Rabindranath from the collective consciousness of Bengalis proved unsuccessful. Notably, some Muslim litterateurs in East Pakistan openly supported the government's stance, expressing their desire to retain Rabindranath in Bengali Literature due to his profound influence.

Historically, Rabindranath Tagore vehemently opposed the creation of Dhaka University, a sentiment shared by the Bengali Hindus of West Bengal who called for the annulment of the Partition of Bengal. This call was eventually heeded on December 12, 1911, leading to the reunification of Bengal. Rabindranath Tagore played a pivotal role in organizing campaigns for the reunification.

The reunification, however, left the Muslims of East Bengal disheartened. To mollify the Muslim League in East Bengal, during Lord Charles Hardinge's visit to Dhaka on January 21, 1912, the Viceroy and Governor-General of India assured Muslim League leaders that a university would be established in Dhaka.

Although East Bengal already had nine colleges, it needed a university to provide higher education. Rabindranath Tagore, influential among upper-class Hindus, expressed his disapproval of the decision to establish a university in Dhaka, formally urging the Viceroy to reconsider.

As a de-facto ruler in Bengal due to his family's extensive Zamindari and widespread respect among the upper-class Hindus, Rabindranath Tagore successfully used his influence to thwart the establishment of Dhaka University despite winning the Nobel Prize in Literature in November 1913. Nevertheless, it was established in 1921 as the University of Dacca under the Dacca University Act 1920 of the Indian Legislative Council. As of today, it is the only oldest active university in Bangladesh.

The intended purpose of Dhaka University, to educate Muslims in mathematics, English, Science, and the Quran, was replaced by a development that cast it as a hostile entity for Muslims in Pakistan and Bangladesh.

From 1968 to 1971, Dhaka University students played a pivotal role in the dismemberment of Pakistan. In 1968, conversations about an independent East Pakistan began, and in 1969, Dhaka University students propagated slogans like "Joy Bangla" and "Joy BongoBandhu," erecting "Aparajeyo Bangla" in 1973.

It is documented that I.B. Agent Serajul Alam Khan orchestrated events leading to the formation of Bangladesh at Dhaka University, specifically in room 108 of Iqbal Hall (now Sergeant Zahurul Haq Hall).

Over a century, Dhaka University's history failed to yield positive outcomes for the Muslim community, instead perpetuating anti-Muslim sentiments. Contrary to the aim of reviving Islamic culture in Bangladesh, the university contributed to the creation of "Aparajeyo Bangla," a symbol that arguably erased Islamic civilization from its grounds. The sculpture work for this symbol commenced at the end of 1973, based on sculptor Syed Abdullah Khalid's design and the supervision of the DUCSU Authority.

Mukti Bahini

After establishing the interim Government of Bangladesh in Calcutta, my blood relative (according to family tradition, nephew, and English tradition, 2nd cousin) was promoted to War General. He was tasked with overseeing the war leadership and gathering strategic operation details. However, he became increasingly frustrated with the Indian defense ministry's interference in his day-to-day tasks. He believed that Indian generals, rather than himself, were primarily responsible for leading the war, while he was merely there for show. He discussed this matter with the Mukti Bahini sector commanders on a few occasions. Their response was resolute, emphasizing that there was no turning back in the current situation except for Pakistan's military withdrawal or the transfer of power. They stressed the necessity of continuing the fight to prevent the loss of millions of lives, including their own.

He came to realize that the war had been thrust upon them by India. He continued in his role as War General until 1972 before assuming the position of Defense Minister. As a former Pakistani colonel, he felt a sense of sorrow witnessing his former colleagues surrender under the command of Indian Generals, their former adversaries. He chose not to participate in the surrender ceremony, knowing that his role would be merely symbolic.

Mujib Bahini

Mujib Bahini was a well-known presence to Dhaka residents from 1948 to 1966. Following the 1946 riot, Mujib envisioned Dhaka as Pakistan's capital and established his influence in the city, leveraging Huseyn Shaheed Suhrawardy's name after Partition.

During the 1971 war, Mujib Bahini, created by Mujib's followers, was organized to wage a guerrilla war against the Pakistani military. I have had the opportunity to meet with Abdur Razzaq twice in my lifetime. The first encounter took place in Sylhet at Hotel Kashmir, where I listened to his accounts of 1971. I covered the cost of his hotel room. The second meeting was in Astoria, NY, where he had become a minister by that time. As I have always maintained, "Bengalis are big fat liars," making it exceptionally challenging to ascertain the truth from them. The involvement of Mujib Bahini in the war remains a highly disputed topic, with the group often being regarded as a criminal gang.

Serajul Alam Khan's visit to India to meet with Prime Minister Indira Gandhi resulted in his request being turned down. Indira Gandhi reportedly deferred to the Indian Defense Ministry, suggesting a reluctance to recognize Mujib Bahini and potentially indicating that it was viewed as a terrorist group.

Mujib Bahini failed to establish itself as a credible freedom-fighting guerrilla group during the war, and instead, it was often characterized as a criminal gang associated with activities such as extortion, rape, murder, and land invasion.

136

Qader Bahini

Qader Bahini was under the complete leadership of Qader Siddiqi and was supported by Golok Bihari Majumder. It functioned as a non-former Pakistani military-trained guerrilla group. Qader Bahini was known to have committed significant war crimes during the war and following the surrender of the Pakistani military.

Communist Revolution

In 1971, the Purbo Banglar Communist Party sought a communist revolution led by Abdul Matin-Alauddin Ahmed but was unable to make a significant impact due to the strong military action from both India and Pakistan. Another major leader of a faction within the Purbo Banglar Communist Party was Tipu Biswas.

Pro-Pakistani Elements

My father repeatedly cautioned me about discussing the Pro-Pakistani elements, a point he emphasized countless times. He served as the "Peace Committee Standing Committee Chairman" during the 1971 war until his passing on February 29, 1992.

I am addressing the topic of Pro-Pakistani elements solely for educational purposes. I've observed that a majority of Bangladeshi Bengalis are unaware of the identity and activities of the Razakers, yet they often denounce them on social media platforms like YouTube and Facebook. Moreover, on the political stage, they vehemently criticize the Razakers, proudly identifying themselves as Bengali and Muktizuddah.

In the late 1980s, various political parties united to overthrow President Hussain Muhammad Ershad. His resignation on December 6, 1990, was not met with the same level of animosity toward former Pro-Pakistani elements. I recall the time when Pakistani cricketer Imran Khan visited Dhaka, and the entire stadium was adorned with the Pakistani flag. However, it's unimaginable to witness the display of a Muslim League flag in Dhaka today.

Upon researching the matter, I discovered that two movements surfaced in the early 1990s: the Bharatiya Dalal Nirmul Committee (Committee for the Elimination of Indian Agents) and the Ekattorer Ghatak Dalal Nirmul Committee (Seventy-one Murderer Brokers Elimination Committee). It became evident that the Ghatak Dalal Nirmul Committee bolstered the Awami League's victory in the 1996 election, while the influence of the Bharatiya Dalal Nirmul Committee waned during the BNP-Jamaat government's tenure.

Many socialists and communists were actively involved in the Bangladeshi entertainment industry, having lost their friends, colleagues, and family members during the Searchlight Operation. The Ghatak Dalal Nirmul Committee stirred Bangladeshi Bengali sympathy through dramas, movies, and music depicting the events of '71. They resorted to falsehoods and fabricated stories to garner support, leveraging Bengali nationalism as a strategic political tool. It's important to note that their political leanings were rooted in socialism and communism, not Bengali nationalism.

Razaker

After its establishment on January 19, 1992, the Ekattorer Ghatak Dalal Nirmul Committee (Seventy-one Murderer Brokers Elimination Committee) in Bangladesh initiated an anti-Pakistan propaganda campaign, fueling animosity through various mediums such as dramas, movies, and music.

When the Awami League assumed power in 1996, it strategically employed the **"divide and rule"** policy, creating a fictitious enemy, the Razaker, to indoctrinate the younger generation. Regrettably, many young individuals now frequently use the term "Razaker" on platforms like YouTube and Facebook, often resorting to offensive language without comprehending its true historical context.

Let me clarify the origins of the Razaker. The Razakar was initially a voluntary paramilitary force established by the Muslim League in June to counter the Mukti Bahini. In contemporary discourse, Bengali speakers often refer to the Pro-Pakistani elements in 1971 as "Razaker" in both news media and social media.

In the early stages of May 1971, the Muslim League leaders faced mounting pressure from the Jobo (Youth) Muslim League and Muslim Chhatru (Student) League to aid in the fight against India and the Mukti Bahini. Consequently, the Pakistan Muslim League and the Pakistan Army agreed to train militia (Razaker) to defend the region and support the military as a supplementary force.

The East Pakistan Muslim League Central Committee passed a resolution stipulating that individuals must possess a recommendation letter from the Muslim League District Committee and complete a Peace Committee information form to be eligible for training in the volunteer militia (Razaker). Subsequently, at the discretion of the Pakistan Army, the individuals underwent military training, ensuring that the process was not open to just anyone.

However, on August 2, 1971, the Governor of East Pakistan, Lieutenant General Tikka Khan, approved an ordinance for the establishment of a voluntary force to be trained and equipped by the Provincial Government. He falsely promised that weapons were en route from the USA, a claim that has been proven to be untrue, as no such shipment ever reached East Pakistan from the USA to this day.

My insights into these events stem from my familial connections. My late father served as the "Peace Committee Standing Committee Chairman" during the 1971 war. Moreover, MAG Osmani was my blood relative and cultural nephew, equivalent to a second cousin in English culture. Additionally, my first cousin held the position of Al-Badr Commander.

In the aftermath of the '71 war and the subsequent general pardon, many Razakers joined the ranks of the Bangladesh Army,

Navy, Air Force, and BDR, representing the initial recruits for these military and paramilitary branches. It is crucial to note that none of the prominent leaders in Bangladesh's political history, including PM/President Sheikh Mujibur Rahman, President Khondaker Mostaq Ahmad, Khaled Mosharraf, President Ziaur Rahman, and President Hussain Muhammad Ershad, initiated any trials for the Razakers. Instead, Razakers served under various administrations in Bangladesh.

It is evident that numerous fabricated stories have been created to vilify the Razakers, reflecting a trend of misinformation and ignorance among many Bangladeshi Bengalis.

Al-Badr

Al-Badr was a prominent pro-Pakistani Mujaheed group, drawing its name from the historic Ghazwat Badr, which symbolized the first conflict between East Pakistan and India in 1971. It is important to note that prior to this, West Pakistan had engaged in several confrontations with India. Ghazwat Badr itself marked the inaugural battle between Muslims and Musrik in Al Madinah.

With my first cousin serving as a notable commander in Al-Badr, I had the opportunity to hear firsthand accounts from him during our family conversations. However, these discussions were always shrouded in secrecy, and as a child, I was cautioned against openly discussing Al-Badr. It wasn't until later in my life that I comprehended the significance of this caution.

To provide some historical context, my cousin completed his BS degree in 1968 in Sylhet and was planning to pursue his MS at Chittagong University. However, at his mother's behest, he decided to take a hiatus and stay with her for a year or two. In the backdrop of the 1970 election, he was situated in Chittagong. One night, my aunt overheard someone in the kitchen and discovered my cousin washing dishes. Upon inquiry, he disclosed the declaration of war by the Major. Alarmed, my aunt sought clarity about the unfolding events, to which my cousin expressed his resolve to engage in jihad against the Musrik and Munafiq. Despite her distress, he assured her of his intentions and left the village, ultimately undertaking numerous operations against the Indian military and the Mukti Bahini. Despite his extensive involvement, he remained unscathed and was never arrested by either the Mujib or Hasina governments. He ultimately passed away, leaving behind a legacy of honor and pure intentions.

In April 1971, my cousin established a contingent of pro-Pakistani and Islamic-minded youth, primarily consisting of college students aged between 19 and 25, under the banner of Al-Badr in Sylhet. The group gradually expanded to include retired army personnel and officers. My father, upon learning of my cousin's involvement, encountered him in a mosque in Sylhet and cautioned him against harming innocent individuals or their relatives, to which my cousin vowed to adhere.

Despite an increased membership of nearly two hundred thousand individuals from Sylhet, Chittagong, Dhaka, Khulna and Comilla Districts, the group needed more weapons. Consequently, Al-Badr resorted to procuring arms from the black market, often obtaining them from Indian sources. This implied that Al-Badr was combating India with weaponry acquired from the same source.

While I cannot definitively ascertain the reasons behind the lack of support from the Pakistani government for Al-Badr, it is plausible that apprehensions regarding potential international censure as a state sponsoring terrorism, inadequate access to weapons, or concerns regarding the group's capacity to confront pro-Indian forces and the Indian Army may have influenced the government's stance.

Al-Shams

I am unaware of the exact origins of the Al-Shams group, but I've heard that "Shams" is a person's name. Whether this is a nickname or the individual's real name, I cannot confirm. It's been suggested that Al-Shams primarily recruited members from various political parties, including the Pakistan Democratic Party, Muslim League (Jinnah), National Awami Party, and Pakistan Socialist Party. Their numbers are estimated to be around one hundred thousand. Notably, they funded their guerrilla warfare using their party funds, without relying on foreign assistance or support from the Pakistan government.

Islamic Jihad or Jundiin Muhammed

Islamic Jihad was primarily composed of qawmi madrasa students, many of whom were from impoverished backgrounds or were orphans. Their funding largely relied on collecting donations from ordinary Muslim families. They were not highly trained or organized fighters. Following the war, a few of them were killed by the Mukti Bahini, while others received threats not to speak in favor of Pakistan in Bangladesh. As a result, they returned to their respective madrasas. In Bangladesh, there is a general sentiment of compassion toward them, which is why they were spared from retaliatory violence. Ultimately, it was widely recognized that Muslim Nationalism was the driving force behind the creation of

Pakistan, and it was understood that the qawmi madrasa students were motivated by emotional, rather than political, factors.

Peace Committee

The Peace Committee represented a fragile unity among the 12 pro-Pakistani political parties with the primary objective of preventing extrajudicial killings by the Pakistani military in East Pakistan and facilitating the repatriation of pro-Indian terrorists. Among the parties involved in the organization of the Peace Committee were Nizam-e-Islam, Jamaat Islami, Pakistan Muslim League, Pakistan Democratic Party, and the National Awami Party. It operated under two names: Nagorik Shanti Committee (Citizen's Peace Committee) and Shanti Committee (Peace Committee). The specific name used was based on party affiliations, with Islamic-minded political parties preferring the former, while both groups operated under the leadership of the Peace Committee Standing Committee.

The Peace Committee's role was to confirm the identities of the accused with their family background and secure the release of pro-Indian terrorists from the custody of the Pakistani military. They also advised the families of the accused to counsel their sons to disassociate from Indian influences and return from any misguided paths they may have taken.

Regarding the 1971 war, it is claimed that the conflict was orchestrated by defected Pakistan military junior officers and financed by the Indian Defense Ministry. The assertion is that India solely managed the war operation financially and in terms of military logistics. No credible evidence has been provided to suggest that Bengali nationalists had organized a well-defined conventional or guerrilla warfare strategy against Pakistan.

Therefore, the entirety of the credit for the victory in the 1971 war is attributed to the Indian military. India's secret war in Bangladesh would have served little purpose without a conventional, disciplined military force, according to this account. The significance and limitations of sub-conventional warfare are cited, emphasizing the importance of studying these tactics closely, as reported by The Hindu on 12-26-2011.

Letter of the Prime Minister of India Mrs. Indira Gandhi to the Prime Minister of Bangladesh Tajuddin Ahmed conveying India's recognition of Bangladesh.

New Delhi, December 6, 1971

Dear Prime Minister,

My colleagues in the Government of India and I were deeply touched by the message which His Excellency the Acting President Syed Nazrul Islam and you sent to me on December 4. On its receipt, the Government of India once again considered your request to accord recognition to the People's Republic of Bangladesh, which you lead with such dedication. I am glad to inform you that in the light of the circumstances which prevail at present Government of India has decided to grant the recognition. This morning I made a statement on the subject in our Parliament. I enclose a copy.

The people of Bangladesh have gone through much suffering. Your young men are engaged in a self-sacrificing struggle for freedom and democracy. The people of India are also fighting in defense of the same values. I have no doubt that this companionship in endeavor and sacrifice will strengthen our dedication to great causes and the friendship between our two peoples. However long the road and however exacting the sacrifice that our two peoples may be called upon to make in the future, I am certain that we shall emerge triumphant. I take this opportunity to convey to you personally, to your colleagues, and to the heroic people of Bangladesh my greetings and best wishes. I should also like to take this opportunity to convey through you to His Excellency Syed Nazrul Islam. Acting President of the People's Republic of Bangladesh, the assurances of my highest esteem.

Yours sincerely,

(Sd.)

Indira Gandhi

His Excellency Mr. Tajuddin Ahmed,

Prime Minister of the People's Republic of Bangladesh, Mujib Nagar.

Chapter Six

14th December

On the fourteenth of December, Bangladeshi Bengali celebrated Martyred Intellectuals Day. I do not have enough information about this day except for knowing that my father left Dhaka early in the morning, and the East Pakistan Government resigned in the morning.

However, during the 1971 war, Pro-Bangladesh Independence journalist Simon Dring was a renowned British journalist. He was in East Pakistan and documented the last days of the war in Dhaka.

Even though Simon Dring was a hardcore supporter of Bangladesh Independence, he never said, "Razaker killed Bengali Intellectual." I have watched his exclusive documentary on the BBC on YouTube. He showed that the Indian Air Force heavily intensified bombardments in Dhaka from early December 4 until December 14, but Bangladeshi Bengali accused the Pakistani military of those air raids.

Secondly, my father was the Peace Committee Standing Committee Chairman. He used to have a full intelligence briefing from the Pakistan military during the war. He also was well-connected with Shah Azizur Rahman. Shah Azizur Rahman led the Pakistani foreign policy delegations to the United Nations from November to December 1971.

Thirdly, the Peace Committee used to have informants in 68 thousand villages in the country. My father was well-informed about International policy and domestic crises.

When General Niazi wanted to continue the war, on December 13, 1971, my father told General Niazi absolutely "No" to continue the fight against India, which would take thousands of innocent lives, and the outcome would be a big zero. Two serious factors developed at the beginning of December 1971. No1, India heavily bombarded Dhaka. No.2 Russia warned the USA that if the US air fleet came to the Bay of Bengal, Russia would bomb the hell out of the USA Air Fleet. Also, in the USA, anti-war sentiment was very high because of the Vietnam War.

Instead, early in the morning, he telegrammed Peace Committee Presidents and Secretaries dated December 14, 1971, in 64 thousand villages, 5 thousand unions, 64 Mohokuma, 16 Districts, and four Divisions. After telegramming all the local Presidents and Secretaries of the Peace Committee, he ran to Kamalapur Train Station to take the 7 or 8 AM train to Sylhet.

The telegram clearly stated," I have a great feeling, by discussing with Sha Azziz, that "by overseeing eight months war, and drunk Yaha Khan leadership, I am certain to a belief that Indian military will march into Dhaka. If they invade East Pakistan, there must be no street resistance, violence, or guerrilla war tactics. We swear on the Quran to protect and secure our people's safety in order to preserve our sovereignty. We failed to defend the sovereignty but the safety of the people on our hands."

My own first cousin was the prominent Al-Badr commander. I never heard from my father or my first cousin in their private conversation that they ever gave an order or advised anyone to kill.

I have seen on the BBC archive that East Pakistan Governor Abdul Motaleb Malik resigned on 14 December 1971 with his entire cabinet and sought refuge in the Red Cross shelter at Dhaka Hotel Intercontinental.

Throughout my life, I have found that Bengalis are pathological liars. Suppose there was any such killing that was obviously done by the Indian Intelligence to prevent any 1971 leaked information. Indian Generals proudly admitted that they had well-organized informants for Indian operations in Dhaka. Bangladeshi Bengali made up and fabricated stories to satisfy their hate for Pakistan.

16 December

The Pakistani Instrument of Surrender was a written agreement documenting 93,000 Pakistani Armed Forces (Eastern Command) on 16 December 1971, ending the Indo-Pakistani War of 1971. The world had witnessed and documented that event.

The Indo-Pakistani War of 1971 was a conventional military war between India and Pakistan that followed during the Pakistan Civil War in East Pakistan from 3 December 1971 to the fall of Dacca (Dhaka) on 16 December 1971.

The war began with the idea of dismembering two Pakistans, East and West, after the Indo-Pakistani War of 1947–1948. It was Indian' interest to dismember Pakistan before it fully integrated as one nation by all means necessary. Politically, it was a crucial decision for India, but morally may not be.

Indian Generals proudly admitted that December 16th was a historic victory for India in two thousand years. And also, after the 2nd World War, it was the first largest military surrender in history. In fear of Pakistan's acts of revenge, Indian Congress political leaders narrate different versions of India's involvement in the Pakistan war. But BJP proudly celebrates India's victory.

Annually, on December 16th, Bangladeshi Bengalis celebrate with pride. I do not remember if anyone celebrated 16

December in my village when I was a kid.

In short, on Thursday, December 16, 2021, India celebrated the 50th anniversary of its victory over Pakistan in the 1971 war that led to redrawing the political map of South Asia and ending the East Pakistan annoyance forever. Moreover, Bangladeshi Bengali celebrated emancipation from Pakistani slavery.

Famous Lie

Bangladeshi Bengalis widely claimed that during the '71 war, the Pakistani military killed three million Bengalis and raped two hundred thousand women during the eight and a half months of civil war. I found this imaginary claim ridiculously absurd. Let us briefly analyze this claim:

No.1: Mujib was arrested at night on March 25, 1971, before the searchlight operation began, and flew to West Pakistan and returned to Bangladesh from Pakistan on January 10, 1972. Mujib publicly said, "I was in a room next to my dug grave." But, the New York Times reported, "The Government released to Pakistani newspapers tonight a photograph that purported to show the East Pakistani leader, Sheik Mujibur Rahman, in police custody at Karachi airport. The photograph shows Sheik Mujib sitting on a sofa in his customary black jacket, flanked by police officers. (NYTIMES 4/11/1971) obviously, a sofa is not a dug grave.

A curious question: How did Mujib know that "the Pakistani military killed three million Bengalis and raped two hundred thousand women," and who gave him this information?

No.2: The so-called Bangladesh Government headquarters was in exile for the rest of the war in Calcutta. When and where did the exiled Government create the independent committee to make a list of dead and raped people?

No. 3: East Pakistan had a functional administrative government until December 14, 1971. To my knowledge, the East Pakistan government never created any committee to list all the war casualties and rape cases.

No.4: My father was the Peace Committee Standing Committee Chairman, who was well aware of the activities of the Pakistani military and Pro-Pakistani elements in East Pakistan. Also, the Peace Committee burnt all the classified information between December 14-16, 1971. I know my father crystal clear under any circumstances. He would never allow killing any innocent person, and rape is beyond imagination. Of course, Bangladeshi Bengali will never understand the moral principles.

No.5: From December 16, 1971, to March 12, 1972, the Indian military was the de-facto ruler of Bangladesh. Indian military did not initiate any war crime investigative committee.

No.6: Officially, the Indian military handed over administrative power to Mujib on March 12, 1972, and my blood relative (according to family tradition, nephew and English tradition 2nd cousin) was War General and Defense minister. As mentioned earlier, none of those administrations made the inquiry and the list of dead and raped people during the war.

Where Bangladeshi Bengali got the information, "the Pakistani military killed three million Bengali and raped two hundred thousand women." A lie that Bangladeshi Bengali invented and believed in it and spreading it. As I always say, "Bangladeshi Bengalis are pathological liars."

Throughout the war, without any doubt, there were thousands of people got killed, including Purbo Banglar Communist, Hindus, Bihari, a few students, Mujib Bahini members, Qader Bahini members, Mukti Bahini Members, Razakers, Al-Badr members, Al-Shams members, Islamic Jihad members, Peace Committee's members, Indian military personnel, Pakistani military personnel, and in cross-border raids some citizens of both countries East Pakistanis and Indians. But, no dead list was ever made.

However, I am not discussing the matter of Shari'a (Islamic Law) in this book. For a basic understanding, rape was a war strategy for thousands of years. When a tribe defeated another tribe, the winner tribe used to take the defeated tribe's girls and women as war booty. Only Islam gradually stopped this evil practice by creating a special status by giving women a choice to revert to Islam or remain as non-Muslims. Non-Muslim women may be considered war booty, but not Muslim women.

Common sense tells us that most of the pro-Pakistani elements were Islamic-minded and believers in Muslim nationalism. They were fighting for the cause of the pan-Islamic identity and Muslim nationalism. They believe that looking at a Muslim woman inappropriately is a sin and a condemnable act. How will they rape their sisters? Of course, every basket of apples has a bad apple.

Historically, after the 1793 Permanent Settlement Act, the rape culture spread in East Bengal by Hindu Zamindars. Thousands of books were written, and hundreds of movies were made about Zamindars kidnapping virgin girls for their sexual satisfaction, raping them, and selling them for prostitution. Islam strictly prohibits this kind of act.

In East Pakistan, from 1948 to 75, rape culture was reintroduced by the Mujib Bahini. Mujib Bahini was forcefully evicting Hindu families, taking their houses, and raping women. Not Islamic groups. In reality, Islamic-minded people execute public beatings for misbehaving with women.

Let us analyze that 93,000 officers and soldiers of the Pakistan Armed Forces were in East Pakistan as of December 16, 1971. It means everyone raped at least two women, and Peace Committee, Razaker, Al-Badr, and Al-Shams, did nothing. They watched rape as porn movies, whereas Mukti Bahini and Indian Army used to urinate on their pants by hearing the name "Al-Badr."

Al-Badr was a pretty well-organized Islamic-minded guerrilla group than the Pakistani military. It was not supported by the Pakistani government like Razaker. If Al-Badr had known anyone raping a Muslim woman, they would have killed the rapiest on the spot because of their Islamic sentiment. They were college and University students, unlike ignorant Madrasa students.

As far as I heard, Mujib Bahini was allegedly raped, targeted, killing Hindus, Bihari, and Pro-Pakistani elements, and acted like a double agent between Pakistan Military and Indian Military. Being a double agent, Serajul Alam Khan interpreted it as a strategic political move to prevent casualties. I am not sure whether he was serious or joking about this statement.

After the war, Mujib Bahini divided themselves into Jatiya Rakkhi Bahini, organized by Mujib Bahini, and Gonobahini, organized by Jatiya Samajtantrik Dal (JSD). They both fought with each other until 1975. Both groups were accused of bank robberies, rape, targeted killings, land invasion, kidnapping, and political assassinations from 1969-1975.

Serajul Alam Khan in NYC admitted he had sex with hundreds of boys and girls in India, Bangladesh, the USA, and East Germany. He does not care about homosexuality or bisexuality.

From the 1990s to this day, their political strategy was to pass all the blame on the former pro-Pakistani elements so that Bengalis would forget about the memory of Pakistan forever.

Bengali Migrants involvement in the 71 War

I am astonishingly surprised to hear about Bengali restaurant workers from the UK who lived on welfare and went to the UK between 1965 and 70 under the President Ayub Khan voucher program agreed upon by the British government. Interestingly, one Voucher forging ten people went to the UK by the PIA during 1965 and 70. In 1971, thousands filed for fake political asylum, capitalizing on the 71 Civil War in East Pakistan. They believed that they made Bangladesh independent by financing the war. My question is, Who did they send money to? Who did they get independence from? They went to the UK through President Ayub Khan's voucher program. He sent manual laborers to the UK from Pakistan, mainly from Sylhet, East Pakistan, because Sylheti people voted for Pakistan in 1947. However, British media called it the Indo-Pak war and separatist movement.

The fact is that the 1971 war between Pakistan and India was a multibillion-dollar internationally known Indo-Pak War and was debated in the UN Security Council. I never heard from the international media that those Bengali welfare recipients and restaurant workers were funding the war. I saw in the international press that Indian Prime Minister Ms. Indira Gandhi said she was financing the war because there was a genocide going on in East Pakistan. And in December, for the first time, she mentioned

Bangladesh. I never saw any UK restaurant workers giving any press briefing about the 71 War. The UK internally wanted to dismember United Pakistan because United Pakistan had changed its dominion status to a sovereign state, which was hard for the British to digest. Cleaning dishes and imagining financing the multibillion-dollar war is a nice dream.

War Crime

My dad told me a few times, "My son, every incident has three stories; never reach a conclusion so fast: No. 1, what people say about the incident that might not be a true narration. No. 2, what people think about the incident might be a guesstimate, not a fact. No. 3, what was the real story? No one knew about it except who was involved in it." That is why verifying the information from the primary source is very important.

As we know, the fact is that every human lies. Finding the truth is difficult because the truth is only one, and people bury the truth with 99% of lies to cover it up.

Naturally, humans are afraid of the truth. They pretend the fact never existed. The truth embarrasses and threatens our credibility in society, so we try to cover it up with 99% lies and deny the truth. The truth is bitter, but it liberates us. Some lies are fun, but they will destroy us.

Bangladeshi Bengali deliberately distorted the history only to cover up their nearly two hundred years being Proza (enslaved people) to Hindu Raja and Zamindars during the British Raj. Bangladeshi Bengali expressed a wave of hatred for former Pro-Pakistan supporters after the Ekattorer Ghatak Dalal Nirmul Committee (Seventy-one Killer Broker Elimination Committee) was created in Bangladesh on January 19, 1992. The committee was formed by 101 Bengali activists led by Jahanara Imam to pursue justice for the "Bengali Genocide" in 1971 East Pakistan during the Pakistan civil war in 1971. They made up a million lies and fabricated stories to hate Razakers, but none had proper knowledge about Razaker. According to them, all former pro-Pakistanis are Razaker. Jahanara's elder son, Shafi Imam Rumi, joined the Communist Revolutionary group, not Mukti Bahini.

During the '71 War, she wrote a diary about the Bengali struggle filled with imaginary fabricated stories that never existed in '71. I have thoroughly researched Western and the USA news. Her "Diary" became one of the most important publications about the War for Bengali Nationalists.

The fact is that her elder son Rumi participated in many guerrilla attacks on the Pakistan army as a Communist, not Bengali. He was arrested by the ISI and never seen again. Jahanara's husband, her younger son Jami, and other male members of the family were also arrested and detained for interrogation. Her husband, Sharif Imam, returned home a broken man, only to die three days before the Pakistani military surrendered to India on December 16, 1971.

I attended one of their meetings in NYC to hear their argument on "War-Crime." They are very aggressive and intolerant of others' opinions and quick to put a label on others. The "genocide" they were referring to that never existed in East Pakistan.

There was a military crackdown on "Violent and criminal gangs" in Dhaka in East Pakistan from March 25 to March 30, 1971, known as "Searchlight Operation." They provided no internationally recognized evidence about the "Bengali Genocide" in East Pakistan except for their pathological lie and made-up story.

On top of that, they believed in a "Western and American" conspiracy to eliminate Bengali. Ironically, they were in the USA. Moreover, many Bengalis legally or illegally migrated to Western Europe and the Americas for a better life.

Historically, Indian Prime Minister Ms. Indira Gandhi first called out "Genocide" after the Pakistan Military conducted a "Searchlight Operation" at Midnight on March 25, 1971, and criticized the USA for supporting United Pakistan's military, followed by the Soviet Union.

However, I gave my opinion to create an "International War Crime Tribunal" with the international communities' guidance and assistance. However, Bengali nationalists rejected it and wanted to use their native judicial process. Nevertheless 2010, the Awami League-led Government of Bangladesh established the International Crimes Tribunal (Bangladesh) to trial war criminals from the Bangladesh Liberation War under an amended version of the International Crimes (Tribunals) Act, 1973. I believe it was a master plan for "judicial" killing to appease the Bengali nationalists for

Awami League political gain.

Let us know what a war crime is. According to International Criminal Law, a war crime is a violation of the laws of War that gives rise to individual criminal responsibility for actions by combatants in action, such as intentionally killing civilians or intentionally killing prisoners of War, torture, taking hostages, unnecessarily destroying civilian property, deception by perfidy, wartime sexual violence, pillaging, and for any individual that is part of the command structure who orders any attempt to commit mass killings including genocide or ethnic cleansing, the granting of no quarter despite surrender, the conscription of children in the military and flouting the legal distinctions of proportionality and military necessity.

As a matter of fact, the 195 Pakistan soldiers who were accused of "War Crime" were released in 1974 without any "Judicial Trial" or "Court Martial." There was also some evidence that 195 soldiers might have committed war crimes. However, senior East Pakistan political parties, including Maulana Bhashani, deemed their release a good gesture to normalize Bangladesh's relationship with Pakistan.

To understand how and why those 195 accused soldiers were released, I have researched the news reports published in international media from March 25, 1971, to April 15, 1974, and also tried to recollect the memories I heard from my father and his friends. In 1971, in East Pakistan, my father was the "Peace Committee Standing Committee's chairman" who used to have complete intelligence briefings from the Pakistan military and the "Peace Committee." My father was a very honest, highly ethical, and moral principle individual. To maintain accuracy, I vetted two categories of evidence, the primary and secondary sources of information.

In the intellectual community, the primary source is more credible than the secondary source. As I am the son of a "Peace Committee Standing Committee Chairman, second cousin (cultural nephew) of "War General" and first cousin of a prominent "Al-Badr" commander, I heard everything firsthand; therefore, I am the most authentic of information on 1971 "Civil War" in East Pakistan.

As the international media, including BBC, reported, in the second week of December, Lt. Gen. A.A.K. Niazi requested the Indian high command for a ceasefire. On December 15, 1971, Gen. Sam Manekshaw, Indian chief of staff, rejected Niazi's request and asked him to surrender by the next day. He assured Lt. Gen. A.A.K. Niazi that the safety of Pakistan's military and para-military forces would be guaranteed. That commitment put the Indian military morally obliged to keep the promise and the Instrument of Surrender legally binding. It means the future "Head of State of Bangladesh" or its judicial system cannot do anything to Pakistan's surrendered soldiers. The point needed to be noted that Pakistan's military surrender to the Indian military was why India had full right to execute its commitment; otherwise, in the eye of the international community would be counted as a failure. To preserve India's high standard in the international community, India did whatever it took to keep its ethical reputation, why Bangladeshi Bengali will never understand in a billion years. Bangladeshi Bengalis are incapable of comprehending the high ethical and moral values due to their two hundred years of being Proza to Hindu Raja and Zamindars.

As the international community witnessed, at the time of surrender, the Pakistani military, under the leadership of Lt. Gen. A.A.K. Niazi, publicly surrendered to the Joint Command of India and Bangladesh known as Mitro Bahini Commander Lt. Gen. Jagjit Singh Aurora (GOC-in-C of Indian Eastern Command.) on December 16, 1971, on the "Instrument of Surrender," Lieutenant-General Jagjit Singh Aurora made a sincere assurance that "personnel who surrender will be treated with the dignity and respect that soldiers are entitled to, following the provisions of the Geneva Convention and guarantees the safety and well-being of all Pakistan military and para-military forces who surrender" based on the Instrument of Surrender written document India can not escape from this legally binding agreement.

The post-war fights erupted, followed by the United Pakistan military surrender to India, among various armed groups throughout the new country "Bangladesh." India's military became alarmed about the safety of the 93,000 POWs and the country's stability. Indian Maj. Gen. Dalbir Singh, who accepted the surrender of some 8,000 Pakistan military personnel in Khulna, his main concern at that time was how to move the POWs to Indian camps as soon as possible and the rapid withdrawal of Indian troops. He said that the Geneva Convention on POWs did not cover the collaborators (Razakers). Bangladesh government will ensure the "Dignity and Safety" of Pro-Pakistani guerrilla groups.

As a matter of fact, Bangladesh's Government was 100% failed to ensure the "Dignity and Safety" of the people, regardless of whether Bengali nationalists or Pakistan supporters and earned an international embarrassment.

Writer Qutubuddin Aziz, in 'Blood and Tears,' has documented 170 eyewitness accounts of the 'atrocities committed on Biharis and other non-Bengalis' across 55 towns, covering '110 places where the slaughter of the innocents took place.' He estimated 500,000 killings by Mukti Bahini.

On December 24, 1971, Bangladesh's Home Minister A.H.M. Kamaruzzaman announced that Bengali authorities had already arrested 30 East Pakistan top Pakistani civilian officials, including Governor Abdul Motaleb Malik, Syed Azizul Huq, Fazlul Qadir Chaudhry, Khan A Sabur, Sultanuddin Ahmad, Abdul Jabbar

Khan, and Pir Mohsinuddin, and would soon put them on trial for genocide. Bengali killed Fazlul Qadir Chaudhry in jail without a trial.

On October 13, 1971, Abdul Monem Khan was shot at his Banani residence by a Mukti Bahini member named Mozammel Hoque.

On March 29, 1972, the Bangladesh government announced a formal plan to try 1,100 Pakistani military prisoners -- including A.A.K. Niazi and Rao Forman Ali Khan -- for war crimes.

At the start, India agreed to hand over all military prisoners against whom Bangladesh presented "prima facie cases" (presenting evidence) of atrocities. However, Bangladesh's Government failed to submit evidence to the Indian Military High Command. As we know, Bengali mobs were killing people in Bangladesh indiscriminately, which they could not expect from India. India was challenged to demonstrate its high moral standards to the international community.

On June 14, 1972, India agreed to deliver 150 POWs, including Niazi, against whom Bangladesh gathered evidence of atrocities, to Bangladesh for the trial. Bangladesh's Government was lacking in evidence. The criminal trial or court martial requires substantial evidence, not hearsay.

On June 19, 1972 -- ten days before the meeting between

Zulfikar Ali Bhutto and Indira Gandhi -- Sheikh Mujibur Rahman reaffirmed his commitment to try 150 soldiers but failed to reach a consensus.

Bengalis' popular belief is that the "Simla Agreement" prevented Bangladesh from prosecuting 150 POWs. The India-Pakistan Simla Agreement was signed on July 2, 1972, which had nothing to do with the "War Crime Tribunal," as I have read it several times.

As I have researched thoroughly with an independent and impartial thought to know the truth, my research showed Bengalis committed atrocity from 1969 to 1975. By the definition of war crime, Bengalis can be tried for the "War Crime." There is mountain evidence against Bengalis. They intentionally looted, raped, targeted killing, political assassinations, and illegally invaded the private property of Hindu, Bihari, Muslim, and Islamic activists. My last word about the "War Crime," as Bengali father Mujib used to say in private conversation, "I can't control these Mad dogs."

The sad truth is that the '71 war was confusing to all political scientists because there was no crystal clear ideological triumph in 1971 for people in East Pakistan (Bangladesh). Mainly, the Awami League fought for a United Pakistan with federalism and provincial autonomy for provinces. Politically, Awami League did not intend to dismember United Pakistan except for these four: Syed Nazrul

Islam, Tajuddin Ahmed, Captain (Rtd.) Mansur Ali and A H M Quamruzzaman. However, the Awami League had five leading factions based on ideological differences. No. 1, All Pakistan Awami League. No. 2, East Pakistan Awami League. No. 3, Awami Bhasani, later known as NAP No. 4, Awami Mujib, known as Mujib Bahini. No.5, Awami Ataur.

The 1968 movement was for democracy against Ayub Khan's dictatorial rule (Muslim League Conventional), not for independence or six points or Bangladesh Independence, but in 1969, Shirazul Alam Khan threw a slogan in the crowd, "Joy Bangla," And Tofail Ahmed threw another slogan "Joy Bongobhandu" that spread throughout East Pakistan and Bengali nationalism capitalized them "Joy Bangla and Joy Bangabandhu."

On May 8, 1966, Mujib was arrested for the Agartala conspiracy, not for the Bengali movement. But Bengali nationalists spread the rumor that Mujib was arrested for Bengali rights. That created atrocity and intensified violence between Bengalis, Beharis, Punjabis, Islamic activists, and Muslim Activists. Behind the scenes, socialists and Purbo Banglar Communists were looting the wealthy families' houses in the name of their fair share.

In 1971, the Purbo Banglar Communist Party wanted a Soviet-type communist revolution in East Pakistan led by Abdul Matin-Alauddin Ahmed, but they failed to have a significant impact because of Indian and Pakistan militaries' iron fist military action against them and local Peace Committees' community work.

In the 1970 election, they all used Mujib, known as the eight-party coalition. Everyone knew Mujib could not control the uprising madness. Bengali madness no one can control. Culturally, Bengalis are highly disrespectful. As of today, 100% of Bengalis have yet to learn that Bangladesh was known as East Pakistan from 1947 to 1971.

In 1955, it was politically named East Pakistan that time, the United Front was in the government, not the Muslim League. Mujib was also in the East Pakistan assembly. There was no objection or protest against it. The East Pakistan and West resolutions were passed without any objection from East Pakistan. The problem was that after the East Pakistan Estate Acquisition Act in 1950, more than Fifteen thousand Rajas and Zamindars left East Pakistan, but their 50 million Prozas, Lathial Bahini, and loyal bureaucrats remained in East Pakistan. They are the major cause of the problem in the country.

Rape 71

"Rape," during the 1971 Civil War in East Pakistan. The fact is that the "Searchlight" operation began at midnight 25th, 1971, for 72 hours to arrest all the rebellious, specifically students (Chhatra League). Approximately 3-5 hundred girls were arrested by the East Pakistan Police, mostly Hindu girls aged between 17-25, more likely college and university students and were politically involved.

As we know, the United Pakistan military started gathering "intelligence" from colleges and universities after January 1971, and the Pakistani military argued that there were high possibilities of preparation for a war in East Pakistan assisted by India, which Mujib categorically denied.

Historically, after the Search Light Operation, 12 Pro-Pakistani political party leaders met with Pakistan's Military High Command to discuss the situation and to understand where the country is heading. After several meetings with the "High Command," the "Peace Committee" was created, and my father was elected as "The Peace Committee Standing Committee's Chairman" after April 8. Almost every Union Presidency and village had a "Peace Committee" before April 16, 1971, and on April 16, 1971, it had the largest rally in Dhaka. The Peace Committee and the Pakistan Military had an intelligence-sharing agreement, which was why my father used to know many things that were happening in East Pakistan.

However, there were some pieces of evidence that girls were raped by Pakistani soldiers, Mujib Bahini, Muktibahin, Qadir Bahin, "Peace Committee's informant," East Pakistan Police, East Pakistan Rangers. Police raped girls during detention interrogation to get information. The raped victims were mostly Hindu girls and some boys, politically involved girls, Bihari, and poor beautiful girls, but no rape victim list was made.

However, Peace Committee burnt all the paper between December 14-16 when India intensified the bombing in East Pakistan. In 1972, my father gave a file to the Mujib administration and requested the government to bring those people to justice. Mujib did nothing.

Shahinul Islam Khalisdar, EA, MST

East Pakistan or Bangladesh

I was asked this question many times during my student life in NYC. As a grandson of the founding member of the Muslim League and son of a late Muslim League leader, it is customary to ask me this type of question to know my opinion. I do not mind if anyone asks me this question. Let me educate you all about my father's stand to answer this question. During the 1971 war in East Pakistan, all the Pro-Pakistani political party leaders elected my father as the "Peace Committee's Standing Committee Chairman." On December 13, 1971, my father deeply thought about all the scenarios in the night. A) Bengal was off and on with India for thousands of years. B) Pakistan was created based on Muslim nationalism; nearly 95% do not know Allah. C) There are dozens of Muslim sects; it is impossible to unite them under Muslim nationalism. D) There was growing regional nationalism. E) There were mushrooming political ideologies. F) There were substantially numbered people alarming poor because of two hundred years of Hindu zamindar slavery.

After carefully thinking about all the factors, in the end, he made up his mind. Early in the morning, he telegrammed Peace Committee Presidents and Secretaries dated December 14, 1971, in 64 thousand villages, 5 thousand unions, 64 Mohokuma, 16 Districts, and four Divisions.

After the telegram, he ran to Kamalapur Train Station to take the 7 or 8 AM train to Sylhet.

The telegram clearly stated," I have a great feeling, by discussing with Shah Azizur Rahman, that "by overseeing eight months war, and drunk Yaha Khan leadership, I am certain to a belief that Indian military will march into Dhaka. If they invade East Pakistan, there must be no street resistance, violence, or guerrilla war tactics. We swear on the Quran to protect and secure our people's safety in order to preserve our sovereignty. We failed to defend the sovereignty but the safety of the people on our hands."This telegram copy was in my father's file until his death. I have read it over a hundred times, but my father told me not to tell anyone. His telegram was a clear indication of accepting India's occupation.

However, on December 16, 1971, the Peace Committee burnt all the war records, and Ms. Indira Ghandi burnt all the War Records in 1972. Also, Bangladesh President Sheik Mujibur Rahman burnt and banned all the newspapers except four in 1974.

That being said, all the memory of East Pakistan was wholly erased. Between 1975-78, all the Pro-Pakistani political parties officially accepted Bangladesh. For the first time in history, the creator of Pakistan's "Muslim League" wrote "Bangladesh Muslim League" in 1978. That's the end of officially East Pakistan. I call it

East Pakistan because my father frequently called it East Pakistan. I do not see any logic in changing the name to East Pakistan. Nevertheless, in 1946, the election was a clear mandate for the creation of Pakistan, and all the East Pakistan political parties uncontestedly passed the 1955 East Pakistan resolution.

There was no anti-East Pakistan movement. Everyone welcomed the resolution except a few West Pakistani political leaders. East Pakistani political leaders argued by creating a two-wing of Pakistan. Pakistan will become much stronger. However, Bangladeshi Bengalis are hardcore believers in Bengali Nationalism, and Bangladesh is their pride.

Chapter Seven
Bangladesh

Who named Bangladesh? This question many people have asked me throughout my life. I am originally from Sylhet. Sylhet was the capital of Assam until the 13th century. Historically, King Gour Govinda was the king of Sylhet. His official language was Nagri, and his religious language was Sanskrit because Mantras are in Sanskrit.

There were thirty tribal kings under his jurisdiction. All Bangladeshi Bengalis do not like to recognize that Sylhet joined Pakistan as a Muslim nationalist by a referendum in 1947. Some Bangladeshi Bengalis aggressively argued that Sylheti is also Bengali. It seems that they will make Sylheti (Assami) Bengali by their own lip service and aggressive poor behavior. Instead, they believed Sylhet was part of Bengal.

Historically, there is no evidence of Sylhet being part of Bengal except for the British creation of East Bengal and connecting the Assam. Bengalis hated Pakistan so much that it seemed they had been enslaved people for Pakistanis for thousands of years. Bengalis' well-established painful argument is that Pakistani raped their mother, sister, and wives and looted their wealth. Historically, Sylhet was the Hindu Kingdom that consisted of thirty petty kings and never gave allegiance to the Sultanate of Sonargaon (Bengal).

179

Bengali culture, language, and politics were different from indigenous Sylheti.

Why am I using the word indigenous? Sylhet was burdened with the influx of Bengali migrants due to the Bengal Famine of 1770, the Bengal famine of 1943, and the 1947 India Partition; those migrants were called "Bengal." I sympathized with Bengali because I saw Bengali bullied in Sylhet daily.

My dad was a Muslim League leader. In 1971, my father was a Peace Committee Standing Committee Chairman. Bengali people curse Razakars, al-Badr, and al-Shams. Their painful memory is that Razakars, al-Badr, and al-Shams raped their sisters, mother, and wives and wanted to eliminate Bengalis.

In 1971, Razakars, al-Badr, and al-Shams were militias fighting against India's military and Bengali separatist terrorists under the supervision of the "Peace Committee." That is why I always sympathized with them. I firmly believe in the idea of Pakistan imposed on Bengali by the Muslim League.

Of course, East Bengali, Sylheti, and Arakani, so-called Muslim politicians, voted in favor of Pakistan's creation, but it seemed to me that most Bengalis disagreed. Muslim League assumed the so-called Muslims in Bengal liked the idea of the Muslim Country Pakistan. However, the disgrace Jinnah made the situation worse. If Jinnah were a sincere Muslim politician, he would have been preparing for Pakistan's the Constitutional Islamic Republic because the Muslim League had stood by the two-nation theory since 1906. On March 23, 1940, the Muslim League passed a resolution to create Pakistan; at that time, the enthusiastic Bengali did not directly oppose Pakistan's creation even though the proposal of the creation of Banglastan was on the negotiating table with the British.

However, in Creation of Bangladesh, Jinnah is 100% responsible. Jinnah always opposed Pakistan's ideas and emphasized Indian Federalism. He was fighting for his 14 points under the Muslim League political banner. In early 1946, Jinnah telegrammed Huseyn Shaheed Suhrawardy that the British Government might not agree to create a new country. Huseyn Shaheed Suhrawardy telegrammed back to Jinnah to keep negotiating with the British negotiators and know that all the options were on the table except dividing the province of Bengal. In mid-1946, Jinnah suddenly declared Direct Action without consulting with the Muslim League cabinet members.

In 1947, Jinnah could have a civil political discussion with the Muslim League cabinet members. Instead, he made his own decision based on the negotiations with the British Counterpart. The weakness of Muslim League cabinet members feared unpredictable Hindu-Muslim bloodshed, which may spill a civil war in British India. And the refusal of the British Government to create Pakistan.

That's why Jinnah found the opportunity to play a monkey business between the Muslim League and the British Government.

My research showed Ishwar Chandra was originally named Bangladesh, and in 1969, Indian agents capitalized on it at Dhaka University under Serajul Alam Khan's leadership. On June 6, 1970, Serajul Alam Khan publicly uttered "Bangladesh" in a student meeting in front of a few students at Dhaka University. According to Indian history, East Pakistan was in a blink of an eye. We must forget about 1947-1971 and let Bangladesh find its own identity. Now, Bangladesh is a reality recognized by the international community.

Sonar Bangla (Golden Bengal)

Many people from India and Pakistan asked me why Bengali sing "Amar Sonar Bangla." My answer is pretty simple. It would help if you asked a Bengali, not me. The second question is, aren't you a Bengali? My answer is simple. In Bangladesh, not everyone is a Bengali; maybe 50-60% of people are indigenous Bengali (Bongo) in Bangladesh.

However, let us check with the historical evidence of Bengal. Impartial historians are still determining the exact origin of the name Bangla. But, Hindu historians believe that the name Bengal, or Bangla, is derived from the ancient kingdom of Vanga (Bongo). References to it occur in early Sanskrit literature. Still, its early history is only possible in the 3rd century BCE, when it formed part of the extensive Mauryan empire inherited by Ashoka.

It was named Sonargaon during the Muslim Sultanate, specifically in eastern Bengal (Bongo). At the time of the East India Company, officially the Presidency of Fort William and later Bengal Province was a subdivision of the British Empire in India.

On July 19, 1905, Lord Curzon announced that Bengal would be divided into East Bengal and West Bengal. Hearing that Bangladeshi Bengali's hearts and minds and highly admired by Bangladeshi Bengali, the son of an East Bengal Zamindar family, Rabindranath Tagore wrote a song, "Amar Sonar Bangla."

The best Bengali of a thousand years ("Hazar Bosorer Srēṣṭha Bengali") were officially Hindu Raja/Zamindar' Proza (Enslaved people) during 1793-1858 under the East India Company Decree known as the 1793 Settlement Act. However, in the dominant Muslim area, they were known as krishak, Maimal, Kamla, etc. From 1858 to 1947, they were under British jurisdiction, characterized as ryiot.

As a reader, you judge and know why it is a Sonar Bangla. Bangladeshi Bengalis believed Bangal was filled with gold, and they were super-rich. And the Muslim invaders and Pakistanis stole all their wealth. The Bengalis viciously hate Muslims.

Bangladesh map

Bangladesh map is the East Pakistan unsettled Map with India. When India was partitioned, Bengal was not partitioned in the name of Bengali nationalism. It was partitioned based on the Hindu Majority and the Muslim Majority theory. Before 1947, East Bengalis were Hindu Zamindars and Rajas' Proza. There were over fifteen thousand Raja/Zamindars in East Bengal, Tripura and Assam.

The borderline was drawn by Law Lord Cyril Radcliffe under instruction from Lord Mountbatten with two legal clauses. No.1 drawn temporary political borderline based on British India districts. No 2, Any British Raja (King) can join India or Pakistan at their discretion. In 1970, Indian Intelligence created a Bangladeshi flag and put the East Pakistan Map inside the flag. In 1972, while printing Bangladeshi Taka, the Bank of India put the Bangladesh Map inside the Taka.

Mujib Government (Between 1972-75)

From 1969-75, East Pakistan (Bangladesh) was in chronic political violence, murder, rape, land invasion, bank loot, robbery, kidnapping, extortion, smuggling, gang violence, Civil-War, coup, counter-coup, and political killing was an ongoing phenomenon. The dead bodies were rotten everywhere in the big cities.

People were dying from starvation, revenge killing, and political assassinations. People were eating soil and leaves, those who were not finding food. Of course, those days were golden times for those who became rich by accumulating wealth overnight through looting and land invasion or gaining bureaucratic positions. For civil society, that was a nightmare. The safety and security of the people were beyond imagination.

From December 16, 1971, to March 12, 1972, the Indian military was the de-facto ruler of Bangladesh. They were struggling to restore law and order in Bangladesh. Bangladeshi Bengali overwhelmingly welcomed the Indian military on December 16, 1971, but the Indian military failed to restore law and order.

In West Pakistan (Pakistan), President Yahya Khan sent a Pakistan International Airline (PIA) flight to bring Bhutto from New York to Pakistan. Bhutto was presenting Pakistan's case before the United Nations Security Council on East Pakistan Crises. Bhutto returned to Pakistan on December 18, 1971.

On December 20, 1971, he was taken to the President's House in Rawalpindi. He took over two positions from Yahya Khan, one as president and the other as the first civilian Chief Martial Law Administrator.

In an AP interview on December 20, 1971, Zulfikar Ali Bhutto clearly said, "I want to keep Pakistan united even if it is a loose federation."

As I gained authentic information in 1998 in Providence, Rhode Island, I ignored it because I was busy with Muslim activism in the USA. I knew the Bengali mentality. They are proud of being Bengali, and 71 is their "Hazar Bosorer Bengali" achievement. They are unwilling to know anything about Pakistan.

According to that source of information, he was a very close aide of Zulfikar Ali Bhutto. He said, " Zulfikar Ali Bhutto and Mujib couple of times had a conversation between December 22, 1971, to January 5, 1972. Mujib promised Zulfikar Ali Bhutto that he would work on creating United Pakistan.

On January 17, 1972, Time reported, Bhutto became President of Pakistan; five days later, he had two meetings with Mujib. Bhutto lived up to his promise. He drove to Islamabad Airport to see Mujib off for London aboard a chartered Pakistani jetliner.

To maintain the highest secrecy, the flight left at 3 a.m. The secret departure was not announced to newsmen in Pakistan until ten hours later, just before the arrival of the Shah of Iran at the same airport for a six-hour visit with Bhutto. Mujib had reached London—tired but seemingly in good health by that time.

New York Times reported on LONDON, Jan. 8, 1972 — Sheik Mujibur Rahman, free after nine months in a Pakistani prison, flew into London today. Last night in Islamabad, Pakistan's new President, Zulfikar Ali Bhutto, kept his promise to let Sheik Mujib leave. He put Sheik Mujib aboard a Pakistan International Airlines plane that arrived here at 6:36 a.m.

However, a few hours later, after talking by telephone with India's Prime Minister Indira Gandhi in New Delhi and with the acting President of Bangladesh, Syed Nazrul Islam, in Dacca, Mujib held a press conference in the ballroom of Claridge's Hotel. While scores of jubilant East Bengalis gathered outside the hotel, Mujib called for the world to recognize Bangladesh, which he described as "an unchallengeable reality," and asked that it be admitted to the United Nations.

However, Mujib shared a similar story to MAG Osmani. He said that he and Zulfikar Ali Bhutto agreed on Federal United Pakistan. Still, when he came to London, he heard that the Pakistan military had surrendered to the Indian Army and the Indian military was in Bangladesh. He was shocked and did not know how to respond to this situation. Also, Bengali in England rejoiced in the defeat of the Pakistani military. He said to MAG Osmani, "Bengali people wanted independence. What can I do?

Sheikh Mujibur Rahman returned to Bangladesh from Pakistan on January 10, 1972. He had stopped in London and New Delhi on his way to Dhaka. He told cheering Indian crowds that his country and theirs would be "bound in eternal friendship as brothers." "The people of India stood by us in our darkest hour, and we will never forget it,"

Lal Bahini (Red Force)

Vanguardism, Lal Bahini (Red Force), was the armed wing of Bangladesh Awami League's labor front Bangladesh Jatio Sramik League (Bangladesh National Labor League) that was active from 1972 to 1975 until the Assassination of Sheikh Mujibur Rahman on August 15, 1975. Bangladesh Jatio Sramik League President Abdul Mannan headed Lal Bahini. The force was basically a vanguard of the then Bangladesh Awami League and was used to suppress the uprising among the workers.

The actual date of the formation of the force has yet to be discovered. Assumebly, it was the underground group who used to commit extortion during 1969-71. Bangladesh's government officially never recognized this group as an official force, but in a public speech, Sheikh Mujibur Rahman called them his Red Horses, who were capable of restoring "Law and Order."

Lal Bahini was dreaded for its ruthlessness in suppressing the non-communist labor protests in the industrial areas of the country, including Tejgaon, Tongi, Adamjee, Kalurghat, and many other places. as well as for fueling riots in the industrial areas. Lal Bahini, Jatiya Rakkhi Bahini, and Shecchashebak Bahini (Red Army, National Force, and Volunteers Force) formed a disgraceful nexus during the Sheikh Mujib regime. Lal Bahini is responsible for hundreds of riots that took place nearly three years and took thousands of lives.

India Bangladesh Friendship

As far as I heard, Mrs. Indira Gandhi assumed Mujib would honor the 71 wartime Indian sacrifices and work on a Confederation Union with India known as "India-Bangladesh Maitree."

The India Bangladesh Maitree dream never came true for Mrs. Indira. Mujib changed his mind when he touched down in Dhaka. MAG Osmani and Major Rab made it absolutely clear to Mujib that the Indian military must leave Dhaka, or the situation would get much more complicated.

Former President of Bangladesh Khondaker Mostaq Ahmad advised Mujib to revoke the "India-Bangladesh Maitree" agreement, which was not legally binding on Bangladesh because Mujib was not in India in 1971.

After Mujib's deep discussion and negation with the Prime Minister of India, Ms.Indira Gandhi and a threat from the Former President of Pakistan, Zulfikar Ali Bhutto, to reclaim East Pakistan in the United Nations, Ms. Indira Gandhi agreed to forge a bilateral agreement and revoke the nonbinding "India-Bangladesh Maitree" agreement which was verbally negotiated with Former Prime Minister of Bangladesh Tajuddin Ahmad in 1971.

On March 12, 1972, the Indian military withdrew from Bangladesh.

The Indira–Mujib Treaty, On March 19, 1972, forged close bilateral relations between India and the newly renamed East Pakistan to Bangladesh. After the signatories of the treaty, the Prime Minister of India, Indira Gandhi and the Prime Minister of Bangladesh, Sheikh Mujibur Rahman. Both declared, "A new friendship has just begun".

Pir Mohammad Habibur Rahman said several times in his conversation after Major Rob threatened Mujib. Mujib called Indira Gandhi and asked her when the Indian military would leave Dhaka. And also, Bhutto continuously contacted Mujib not to make any consensus with India until the situation settled down.

From my desk

As I have thoroughly researched the Bengali claim regarding the Greatest Bengali and Pakistanis making Bengali slaves, in short, I conclude with this: on December 16, Vijay Diwas (Victory Day) is observed every year to honor the victory of the Indian armed forces against United Pakistan in the 1971 war. Indians pay tribute to the soldiers who sacrificed their lives to defend the honor of India. India secured a historic triumph over Pakistan on December 16, 1971, leading to the renaming of Bangladesh from the former East Pakistan.

Bengali Wins Freedom

On this Newly formed Union of India, General Amir Abdullah Khan Niazi, the head of United Pakistan's armed forces, along with 93,000 soldiers, made a historic surrender to the Indian Army, marking a landmark military surrender post World War II. India reflects on the sacrifices made by the defense forces During the 1971 war on this day. But, Bangladesh Bengali celebrates December 16 as " ("The best Bengali of a thousand years").

In short background history, in 1947, a blunder mistake was made by partitioning the British Raj into two Union of India and Pakistan on the religious lines Hindu and Muslim. Since then, India and Pakistan engaged in a couple of Wars. It was politically important for India to dismember United Pakistan. Also, in East Pakistan, Bengali nationalists were feeling contentious under the Muslim nationalization.

The Bengali nationalists instigated the 1971 war, and Sarbadaliya Chhatra Sangram Parishad was a student organization that was formed to demand 11 points and the resignation of Ayub Khan, mainly consisting of Communists, Socialists, Secularists, and Bengali Nationalists, led by Noor Alam Siddiqui, Abdul Kuddus, A S M Abdur Rab and Shajahan Siraj.

The origin of the movement was on January 4, 1969, when left wing students organized. The joining of the East Pakistan Student Union (Matia), East Pakistan Chhatra League, East Pakistan

Student Union (Menon), and the Dhaka University Student Union. The student demanded Eleven Points, which was based on the 1965 Six Points of Sheikh Mujibur Rahman and the Awami League (Mujib).

The students called for a strike on January 20, 1969 throughout East Pakistan. Amanullah Asaduzzaman, a student, was killed by police, which led to more strikes, demonstrations, and violence from 21 to January 24.

On January 24, 1969, the violence intensified; two more protesters were killed in Mymensingh by police. Many were injured throughout the East Pakistan. East Pakistan was shaken by violence. Approximately 61 people were killed during the intense violence that was the beginning of a vicious culture of violence until 1975.

The 71 Indo-Pak War did not end the cycle of Bengali violence culture that continues to this day. The question arises: what was it all about? Still, India has over a hundred million Muslims, and Bengalis are still in the cycle of violence.

President Zia and BNP

In a Restaurant in Dhaka in 1975, my father said to Shah Azizur Rahman, "The country is bigger than the Party, and the Party is bigger than individual interest." when he was advising Shah Azizur Rahman to back up Zia to build the country.

Many people have asked me to join the BNP more than a few times. My response was that my father chose the USA for us, not Bangladesh or Pakistan. However, I do know who Zia Ur Rahman is and about the formation of BNP.

In the initial stage of the BNP, there was a strong vetting process to recruit party leadership. Only ethically moral principles individuals were invited to join the party. Obviously, there was no chance for crooks in BNP. After President Zia's assassination, everything changed, and some left the BNP.

Bengalis are pathological liars. They invented thousands of lies about Major, General, or President Zia. Historically, President Zia was a very professional, ethical, intelligent, brave, honest, and straightforward person. Individually, he never favored anyone. General Zia came to power by 100% socialist Muktibahini and Razakers. On November 7, 1975, the Bangladesh coup was a coup d'état launched by left-wing army personnel in collaboration with left-wing politicians from Jatiya Samajtantrik Dal.

The coup resulted in the death of Major General Khaled Mosharraf, who, only three days prior, led a coup against those involved in the assassination of Sheikh Mujibur Rahman.

During the coup, Ziaur Rahman was freed from house arrest, enabling him to seize power and become president. Socialists believed General Zia would declare "Socialism" in the country, but before that, my father and MAG Osmani negotiated with him to remain neutral until the situation calmed down and the plan would be executed.

General Zia respected the advice and played neutral until, politically, the BNP was formed in 1978. President Zia never invited anyone to join the BNP. There was an advising body behind the scenes before forming BNP. The advising body used different techniques to invite people to join with BNP. Their objective was to unify the country and stabilize it from the ongoing violence and coup and counter-coup.

One of the leading advisers was my father. My father would never know today's idiots in the party. These bastards think it was a joke to save a country from anarchy, atrocity, chronic violence, coup, and counter-coup just by making Zia a war hero. No, making Zia a war hero, the chronic violence that started in 1969 would never stop because there were dozens of groups fighting with each other.

These bastards ate too much panta bhat. That was why their

brains did not work except for "joy Bangla, joy Bangabandhu."

In short, Zia Ur Rahman was a junior Pakistan Army officer. He was the bravest Army officer during the 1965 war between Pakistan and India. He also performed some Pakistan ISI tasks.

In 1971, Zia Ur Rahman was posted as an Army Major in East Pakistan, Chittagong. As a former ISI task officer, he knew East Pakistan faced a profound existential crisis. During 1971, the political situation was unpredictable and uncertain in East Pakistan. East Pakistan needed an acceptable decisive political leader who could decisively lead the nation.

As a reminder, the entire Pakistani population has been dissatisfied with the government of Pakistan since its creation, disregarding West Pakistan or East Pakistan. The day Pakistan was created, Pakistan was paralyzed in political, ideological, tribal, and religious gridlock.

The stability of Pakistan was under a big question mark because there was no precise political solution in the country. Instead of people liking Pakistan, they started cursing Pakistan. Zia Ur Rahman knew these issues because he came from a highly educated Muslim family and a former Malik family.

On March 25, 1971, he could not control his moral consciousness when he sensed the Pakistani military would kill many innocent people in the name of a Searchlight Operation in East

Pakistan. He spontaneously decided

to "revolt" and to declare the "Independence of Bangladesh."

As a military officer, he knew breaking the chain of command and revolting against military command could cost his life. He put his life at risk and declared the "Independence of Bangladesh."

The official Mukti Bahini was organized under my nephew's (In English tradition, 2nd cousin) leadership, MAG Osmani, in late April 1971. Zia Ur Rahman was appointed as a sector commander under my nephew's command.

MAG Osmani was a former retired Pakistan Army colonel. MAG Osmani personally asked Zia Ur Rahman to know if he declared "Independence" under the influence of the RAW agent. He always denied participating in the "RAW" master plan. He repeatedly told MAG Osmani that his natural instinct told him to do that. MAG Osmani asked him, "Did Mujib influence that?" Zia Ur Rahman repeatedly reaffirmed that he is a professional soldier, not a politician.

By the way, MAG Osmani contested the 1970 election against my father. He defeated my father with landslide votes. My father ran as a Muslim League candidate, and Osmani ran as an Awami (federalist, not Mujib) candidate. My father used to say, "It was a rigged" election. He used to smile and say, "I did nothing; I was drinking my coconut water and coffee, reading a book, listening to the Radio."

In the early morning of August 15, 1975, my mom would visit my step-sister. She noticed something that seemed odd. She asked the driver what was going on. The driver told my mother, "Ma'am, 'Pharaoh died.'" Bangladesh was on an unknown horizon from August 15, 1975, to November 7, 1975. No political expert was able to assess the situation.

On August 15, 1975, Khondaker Mostaq Ahmad immediately took control of the government after Mujib's assassination, proclaiming himself President. Major General Ziaur Rahman was appointed Chief of Army Staff of the Bangladesh Army, replacing K. M Shafiullah.

On November 3, 1975, the Pro-Indian Mukti Bahini staged a coup against President Khondaker Mostaq Ahmad, accusing him of Islamizing Bengali. My nephew, MAG Osmani, protected him from the coup.

On November 7, the socialist Mukti Bahini group staged a counter-coup against Pro-Indians and released General Zia from house arrest. As a matter of fact, the socialist Mukti Bahini misunderstood Zia Ur Rahman. Zia Ur Rahman came from a deep-rooted traditional Muslim family, unlike most typical religious ignorant Bengali.

After Zia Ur Rahman became Head of the State, my father

went to MAG Osmani's house in Sylhet. My father, MAG Osmani, Colonel (Major) Rab, and Major (Captain) Farid Uddin discussed the country's future all night. After Fazr's Prayer, MAG Osmani started calling whomever he felt trusted and reliable to stand behind Zia.

On the other hand, my father started calling all the Islamic-minded Muslim leaders and Razakar commanders to stand behind Zia. As my father was "Peace Committee Standing Committee Chairman," he knew the reliable commanders.

Between 1975 and 78, my father convinced a faction of Muslim Leaguers, Nizami Islami, the former Pakistan Democratic League, and many other former Pakistan political parties to support Ziur Rahman's sake of Allah to rebuild the country.

To the best of my memory, I heard Zia Ur Rahman was a brave, honest, intelligent young man. He was mindful of being a Muslim and worked hard to unite Razakers and Mukti Bahini. He risked his life to integrate Razakars, and Mukti Bahini and confronted India.

The present BNP is corrupt and aimless. They failed to protect former Razakers such as Halim and Salauddin. Etc. And Mujib killers. The former pro-Pakistani political parties' sons and grandsons will never trust BNP.

Bangladesh Economy

Over the past fifty years, Bangladesh's economy has grown enormously. Bangladesh's economic freedom score is 52.7, making its economy the 137th freest in the world in the 2022 Index. Bangladesh is ranked 29th among 39 countries in the Asia–Pacific region, and its overall score is below the regional and world averages. Pakistan's economic freedom score is 48.8, making its economy the 153rd freest in the world in the 2022 Index. Pakistan is ranked 34th among 39 countries in the Asia–Pacific region and its overall score is below the regional and world averages. (Source www.heritage.org/) Pre-1947, the East Bengal economy was in the hands of more than fifteen thousand Hindu Zamindars. And their Banking reserve was in Calcutta. They heavily industrialized Calcutta but nothing in Dhaka or Sylhet. First, Calcutta was British India's capital for nearly one hundred fifty years. Secondly, the provincial capital of Bengal. During the partition negotiation between Lord Mountbatten and Jinnah, Lord Mountbatten was under pressure from the Bank of England not to give Calcutta to Pakistan. And also, the wealthy Hindu establishment strongly opposed the transfer of Calcutta to Pakistan.

Last two hundred years, London has been a direct business partner with Calcutta. The high volumes of financial transactions between Calcutta and London were at stake. That's why there was a mountain of pressure on Lord Mountbatten not to hand over Calcutta to Pakistan. Lord Mountbatten played the same trick as Lord Clive did in 1757. Lord Mountbatten lured Jinnah to make him a Governor-General of Pakistan, and King George VI became King of Pakistan, a title Jinnah had obsessed with since childhood. The power transfer was in Karachi, a small town compared to Calcutta, Lahore, or Dhaka. Jinnah accepted the deal in a closed-door meeting with Lord Mountbatten without consulting with Muslim League Cabinet Members and without understanding the financial consequences that the new country would face. The title "Governor-General" appealed to Jinnah more than the country and its people. On the day of the power transfer, almost all senior Muslim Leaguers were shocked. They received the information through a telegraph that Lord Mountbatten and Jinnah agreed on the creation of Pakistan. There were no details on how to prepare for the partition. Lord Mountbatten played a psychological game with Jinnah and got the job done on behalf of the Bank of England.

On August 14, 1947, East Bengal was on an unknown horizon. The exact situation of the partition was still being determined. Lord Mountbatten left a map in the hand of Jinnah. Once again, Muslims in Bengal were deceived by another Mir Jafar. Muslim League was not prepared for this financial challenge and massive migration. However, the Bank of Lahore set up the Pakistan Banking system and created cash flow into the economy at the beginning of 1948. As fifteen thousand Hindu Zamindars converted their assets into Indian Rupees, that was a sound alarm to the Muslim League leaders. All the political parties in East Bengal unanimously voted for the East Bengal State Acquisition and Tenancy Act of 1950, which created more than a couple million landowners and made more than fifteen thousand Hindu Zamindars poor. The 1950 Land Reform Act did not benefit the poor people as the politicians in East Bengal thought. The former Hindu Zamindars' employees and **Lathial Bahini** took full advantage of the new law. They were well aware of Zamindars' assets and deeds and were well connected with the legal professional, making it easy for Zamindars' employees and **Lathial Bahini** to take those Hindu Zamindars' assets.

During 1948-1958, Pakistan was under ideological gridlock. The Muslim Nationalists dominated Sylhet, Dhaka, Chittagong, and Comilla districts. The North and South Bengal were overwhelmed by the socialists' and communists' political and ideological activists who were experiencing extreme poverty in that region. On the other hand, West Pakistan was filled with tribal and religious tension between Hindu minorities, Shia, Sunni, Hanifi, and Barelvi. There was no political or economic settlement at this time in Pakistan. Pakistan's economy was growing because of the wealthy families' private investment in the Jute Factories, Sugar Factories, Paper Mills, Textiles, Sawmill, Rice mills etc. In 1958, the Military took over, and President Ayub Khan laid a master plan to lead Pakistan in the 21st century. He built a good relationship with Muslim Leaguers and wealthy families known as 22 families. His vision was that before 1980, Pakistan would defeat Japan in the economy. Between 1958-66, Pakistan grew on the fast track of the economy and education that shocked the world. The basic Democracy plan created nearly five thousand small towns and made millions of businesses and jobs. The Basic Democracy Union Presidency helped build primary, high school, and post offices in remote areas. The blunder mistake of the 1965 war was disastrous for United Pakistan. It did affect East Pakistan's economy significantly. With the ongoing violence between 1967 and 1971, Pakistan's economy was unsustainable. It was on the brink of collapse. The political unrest created panic in the economy. The economy of Pakistan was in turmoil; wealthy families converted their assets to U.S. dollars and U.K. pounds. At some point in East Pakistan, Bengali nationalists built an argument on "Economic discrimination and disparity" between East Pakistan and West Pakistan and claimed Pakistanis discriminate against Bengalis. Awami League capitalized on "Economic discrimination and disparity" and emphasized on Provincial Autonomy. Awami League politically was not a Bengali nationalist party. It was a Federalist party, but Serajul Alam Khan intended to make Awami League a Bengali nationalist party. He threw a "Joy Bangla" slogan in 1969 at the anti-Ayub movement that spread everywhere in East Pakistan.

Bengali Wins Freedom

From 1950 to 1971, Pakistan's main export was jute, but Private companies owned all of the Jute Mills and were not publicly owned. Adamjee Jute Mill was a jute mill in East Pakistan. It was established in Narayanganj in 1950 by the **Adamjee Group**. It was the first jute mill in East Pakistan, the largest jute mill in the world, exceeding the jute mills of Calcutta, India, and Dundee, Scotland. The Jute mills were enviously nationalized by Mujib in 1972, including my father's textile mill. Mujib renamed it The Bangladesh Jute Mills Corporation, and it was operational before closing in 2002. From 1972-75, the Mujib Government enviously and jealously nationalized everything, like the Soviet Union, without declaring a Communist Revolution.

Mujib Bahini stole all the machines from textiles and sold the devices on the Indian black market. The economy totally collapsed, hyperinflation hit the market, and crime skyrocketed. Foreign investors ran away from a newly renamed East Pakistan to Bangladesh. The problem in the mind of Bengalis was that they needed to understand the difference between private-sector investment, public-sector investment, and foreign exchange. However, Bengali argued that Pakistan was investing in West Pakistan heavily. This argument was the fact. Pakistan's Central Government invested 55% to 60% from 1950 to 1971 in West Pakistan, and East Pakistan generated 70% of the foreign exchange. Generally, the private sector is owned by corporations, partnerships, or sole proprietorships. To generate revenues, a government can only impose taxes on the private sector, nothing more. If jute and tea generate 70% of foreign exchange, how much can a government collect taxes from them? These factors Bengali could not comprehend. If I remember correctly, I heard the logic behind investing in West Pakistan for two reasons: No.1: West Pakistan's land size was bigger than East Pakistan, and the population was small. East Pakistan's Land size was small and overpopulated; in the monsoon seasons, it flooded. The idea was to gradually relocate some people to West Pakistan to reduce the burden on East Pakistan. Naturally, people only like to move from their parent's house once they see an opportunity. Of course, no one likes to take poor people. Everyone feels poor people are a burden and a liability. Creating opportunities requires lots of investment. That's what Bengali did not understand.

No.2: in 1956, Pakistan declared its independence from the British Crown under Muslim League leader Mohammad Ali, ended its dominion status to sovereignty, and adopted a Republican Constitution in 1956, publicly establishing Pakistan's Islamic Republic that left the British Crown and Soviet Union unhappy which required more investment in the defense.

East Pakistan did not have Military training facilities due to the British ban in 1858, but West Pakistan did have Military Training Facilities.

Bengali Wins Freedom

Pakistan Prime Minister Mohammad Ali Bogra created the One Unit Governmental System, which unified the four western provinces into a unit called West Pakistan. At the same time, East Bengal was renamed East Pakistan. Interestingly, not a single East Bengali political leader, intellectual, or common person objected to renaming East Bengal to East Pakistan. Not even Bangladeshi Bengali Father Mujib.

The critical political problem was the equal distribution, which was impossible because East Bengal/ East Pakistan had a significant overpopulation and small land. If we analyze the scenario of the State of Pakistan, it has four provinces in the west and only one thousand miles away in the East. If we divide 100 by 5, East Bengal gets only 20%. If we analyze the scenario of the Islamic Republic of Pakistan, West Pakistan had 12 divisions, and East Pakistan had three divisions. Let us divide 100 by 15 per division qualified for 6.66 %. If we multiply 6.66 by 3, East Pakistan only allowed for 20%. No political genius can resolve this political problem except by declaring the Independence of East Pakistan or Autonomy like the USA.

On April 7, 1972, after the 71 War and the eventual creation of Bangladesh's governmental administration. The country's central bank and the main regulatory body for Bangladesh's monetary and financial system were created with the help of India. The Government of Bangladesh passed the Bangladesh Bank Order,

1972 (P.O. No. 127 of 1972), reorganizing the Dhaka branch of the State Bank of Pakistan as Bangladesh Bank. Bangladeshi Taka was connected with the Indian Central Bank and the Rupee. The official introduction of the Taka was on March 4, 1972, in India. India politically put a map inside the Taka so that the Bangladesh government cannot reclaim the disputed areas in the future. During 1972-75, Bengalis were dying from starvation. Two Muslim Leaders helped Bengalis, King Faisal bin Abdulaziz and Sheikh Zayed bin Sultan Al Nahyan. At the end of 1975, at the request of Shah Azizur Rahman, they injected a couple of hundred million dollars into the Bangladesh Bank for Foreign Reserve. Between 1975-78, my father and Shah Azizur Rahman met a few times in Dhaka to discuss the Muslim League's future with many other Muslim Leaguers. My father said, "It is naïve to believe that East Pakistan and West Pakistan will ever become a United Pakistan." "It is better to make Bangladesh Muslim League." However, in a restaurant, my father told Shah Azizur Rahman. "Muslim League does not have a future in this country." "If Zia invites you to join with him, join." "Use your political experience and knowledge for these poor people. Sake of Allah." He looked at my father with a surprised look. He said, Lal Saab, you are the boss and a sincere senior leader. I respect your opinion and will think about it." President Zia invited **Shah Azizur Rahman** to join with BNP. Shah Azizur Rahman accepted the offer to join BNP; President Zia made him a labor minister. He made some robust labor reforms to boost the economy. He advised President Zia to build a stable relationship with Muslim countries. Shah Azizur Rahman reshaped the foreign and economic policy of Bangladesh. President Zia, King Khalid bin Abdulaziz, and Sheikh Zayed bin Sultan Al Nahyan signed a kafil system to send Bangladeshi to Gulf Countries; the scheme's architect was Shah Azizur Rahman. Today, Bangladesh is a product of political genius Shah Azizur Rahman., not Mujib.

In the late 90s, I met the former finance minister Mohammad Saifur Rahman. He and I talked in a restaurant in NYC for a couple of hours. When we were deep into the economic discussion, he asked me what could be done differently. I called the waiter to give me the bill for our table. The waiter came with the bill. I showed him the bill. I took my wallet out to pay for the bill. He said, "NO." But I paid. I asked him, "Sir, what did you see? He asked, "Where?" I said, "Sir, you are an economist, and you have seen nothing." I explained to him that I said, " Sir, first, we came to the restaurant. We sat on the chairs. A waiter came and asked for the order of food. No one knows why we came to this restaurant, but the waiter, indirectly with a smiling face, told us to spend money to sit there. That's the modern-day economy.

The economic thinking about a human as a consumer or a worker that is called the modern economy. Secondly, I explained to him, "I expensed, and you saved." Socially, it's honorary hospitality but economically "save and expense." In Bangladesh, the economy needs lots of foreign reserves to cut imports. Increase the exports. And also create a mechanism to collect taxes. He smiled and said, "Mirasdari blood." Thank you! I learned a lot.

Islamic Revolution in Bangladesh

In September 2001, I discussed this issue with Amir of Jamaat E Islami Bangladesh, Professor Ghulam Azam, for approximately two hours in NYC. In Bangladesh (East Pakistan-1955-1971), Jamaat E Islami worked for a democratic Islamic revolution for nearly 60 years in Bangladesh (East Pakistan). As a grandson of a Muslim League founding member and son of a late Muslim League leader, I warned him, "That will never happen in Bangladesh in the next billions of years." I reminded him, "Pakistan was the first country born under the banner of Muslim nationalism; it could not survive twenty-three years. Pakistan has been a curse to many people and has been politically unstable since its birth.

However, the creation of Pakistan created one of the lies of Bengali Nationalism in East Pakistan, and you are one of the leading Bengali Nationalists. Recently, you converted to Muslim Nationalism." I told him, "Emotion and knowledge are not the same things. They are pretty much different from each other."

Historically speaking, the 1793 Permanent Settlement Act of East India Company created the village-to-village autonomous petty governmental system with East India Company loan and gun power assistance. The non-Muslim petty village rulers banned Masjid and Islamic education until the British Government lifted the ban in 1858.

Hindu Zamindars used Lathyal Bahini to suppress Muslims and invade Muslim land. Most of the Lathyal Bahini recruited poor Muslims by luring them with better payments and tax-free housing. Between 1793 and 1858, their name was changed; some of them even forgot their Islamic celebration.

Before the Muslim League's creation in 1906, the Muslim upper class and middle class published a book for Muslim names and distributed the book from village to village. Between 1930 and 37, for the Census of India 1931, the Muslim League created a voting list for the 1937 Bengal Provincial election and changed many Bengali names to Muslim. Almost all male first names were listed as Muhammed, and female last names as Begum or Khatoon.

In 1858, the British Government introduced the British medium educational system with the promise of civil service jobs. As most Muslim middle-class race to competitively get British jobs, they ignored Islamic education.

After the 1906 formation of the Muslim League, the privately operated Madrassa began in Muslim-dominated areas. Those Madrassas are producing unskilled Mullahs, which are seriously dangerous for society. I firmly believe it is time for the Muslim community to educate themselves about monotheism, five times prayers, and train them to work in agriculture, technology, medicine, etc. The suicide bombs on innocent people, violence on the street, and cursing the rulers will not benefit anyone; instead, they will give bad names to Muslims and make Dawa's work much more difficult. Today, Muslims are religiously ignorant, bureaucratically corrupt, culturally criminal minds, etc. I believe it is time to come to our senses and spread correct Islamic Aqidah. Not the Islamic revolution.

Conclusion

In conclusion, I have experienced the Bengali nationalists' abusive behaviors toward Muslim activists in Bangladesh. I assume it is a pretext to take sympathy from the Bengalis for political gain. However, the mistake was already made in 1906, 1946, and 1971. These mistakes cannot be corrected by returning back to the dates. Cursing Razaker, Al-Badr, and Al-Shams will not benefit the country.

The people in the country are heavily suffering from injustices, loot, rape, murder, fraud, thieves, land invasion— political instability. It is time for the new generation to rethink. Should they stick with Bengali and Pakistani hatred or move forward as a unified Bangladeshi?

It is ridiculous to believe that Bangladesh and Pakistan will ever be united. As a United Pakistan, it survived only for 23 years with political instability, cultural inferiority, and ideological gridlock. Compared to India's Bengal history, it was just a blink of an eye.

In reality, Bangladesh is an internationally recognized country and a member of the United Nations (U.N.). It is overpopulated, condensed at 160 million people, and one of the world's poorest countries. The Government of Bangladesh cannot afford to engage in a conventional war against any external enemies.

The country should create a confederacy union with the neighboring countries, especially with India. In this current geopolitical and overpopulation crisis, the alleviating poverty dream of the past.

Bangladesh needs to have a master plan to tackle the internal political, social, economic, religious, and educational disturbances. The Government of Bangladesh must prioritize eliminating criminalistic culture to ensure all Bangladesh citizens' safety and security, disregarding political, religious affiliation, and social hierarchy, and restore the ethical culture. That will increase the country's reputation and lure investors into investing in the economic sectors. The quality of life of people will habitually improve with the flow of financial vibration.

Last word:

By Al-`Asr. Verily, man is at a loss. Except those who believe and do righteous deeds, and recommend one another to the truth, and recommend one another to patience. Al-Quran 103:1-3

Further Reading

1. *Indian Political Thought, Sharma, Urmila; Sharma, S.K. (2001), Atlantic Publishers & Distributors, ISBN 9788171566785*

2. *Caste: The Origins of Our Discontents* – By Isabel Wilkerson, Publisher: Random House (August 4, 2020).

3. *India's External Intelligence: Secrets of Research and Analysis Wing RAW* – By V.K. Maj. Gen. Singh, Manas Publications (July 30, 2007).

4. *India Wins Freedom* – By Maulana Abul Kalam Azad, Publisher: Sangam Books Ltd; 1st edition (December 1, 1998).

5. *Jinnah: India, Partition, Independence* – By Jaswant Singh, Publisher: Oxford University Press; 1st edition (February 28, 2010).

6. Conflict Diplomacy: The U.S. and the Birth of Bangladesh Pakistan Divide – By Jaswant Singh, Publisher: Rupa Publications India (February 1, 2008).

7. *Democracy And The Challenge Of Development (A Study of Politics and Military Intervention in Bangladesh)* – By Moudud Ahmed, Publisher The University Press Limited, Red Crescent Building, 114 Motijiheel c/o P.O Box 2611, Dhaka 1000, Bangladesh.

8. *Bengali Politics Documents of the Raj*, Editors: Enyetur Rahim, Joyce L. Rahim, Publisher The University Press

Limited, Red Crescent Building, 114 Motijiheel c/o P.O Box 2611, Dhaka 1000, Bangladesh.

9. *The Betrayal of East Pakistan* – By A. A. K. Niazi, Oxford University Press, Feb 24, 2000.

10. *Islamic Economics, Theory And Practices, A Comparative Study* – By M.A. Manan, Printed 1991, Sh. Muhammed Asaraf, Publishers, Booksellers & Export, 7 Aibak Road, New Anarkali, Lahore, Pakistan, Associated Press AP Archive.

Websites:

- https://www.rct.uk/collection/themes/publications/eastern-encounters/chapter-1

- https://www.nytimes.com/1972/01/11/archives/mujib-stopping-in-new-delhi-vows-eternal-amity-with-india.html

- https://www.nytimes.com/1972/03/13/archives/indias-soldiers-quit-bangladesh-ceremonies-in-dacca-mark-pullout.html

- https://www.britannica.com/

- https://sourcebooks.fordham.edu/india/1617englandindies.asp

- https://en.wikipedia.org/wiki/Main_Page is a community of volunteer contributors, and anyone can change the information from Wikipedia.

- http://bdlaws.minlaw.gov.bd/act-details-415.html?lang=bn

- https://www.youtube.com/watch?v=KWEP7XbO6H8

- https://www.youtube.com/watch?v=X2d872sKV2o

- https://www.youtube.com/watch?v=FuirDA3NK5I

- https://nvdatabase.swarthmore.edu/content/pakistanis-demand-their-government-recognize-bengali-official-language-1947-1952#:~:text=Victory%20finally%20came%20on%207,official%20state%20languages%20of%20Pakistan.

218